D1147667

Plays: 1
The No Boys Cricket Club, Starstruck, Lift Off

The No Boys Cricket Club: 'A fascinating psychological study of a woman coming face to face with her former self, gaining power from her cultural roots and eventually realising that the two distinct parts of her life make up a whole woman.' *What's On*

Starstruck: 'A quirky comedy . . . soon darkens and mutates into a tragic vision of incestuous family life, soiled dreams and the rude wisdom of having to make a virtue of necessity.' *Evening Standard*

Lift Off: 'Williams's writing snaps and crackles, his characters burst with life, emotion and contradiction.' *Guardian*

Roy Williams worked as an actor before turning to writing full-time in 1990. He graduated from Rose Bruford in 1995 with a first class BA Hons degree in Writing and participated in the 1997 Carlton Television screenwriters' course. *The No Boys Cricket Club* (Theatre Royal, Stratford East, 1996) won him nominations for the TAPS Writer of the Year Award 1996 and for New Writer of the Year 1996 by the Writers' Guild of Great Britain. He was the first recipient of the Alfred Fagon Award 1997 for *Starstruck* (Tricycle Theatre, London, 1998), which also won the 31st John Whiting Award and the EMMA Award 1999. *Lift Off* (Royal Court Theatre Upstairs, 1999) was the joint winner of the George Devine Award 2000. His other plays include: *Night and Day* (Theatre Venture, 1996); *Josie's Boys* (Red Ladder Theatre Co., 1996); *Souls* (Theatre Centre, 1999); *Local Boy* (Hampstead Theatre, 2000); *The Gift* (Birmingham Rep/Tricycle Theatre, 2000); *Clubland* (Royal Court, 2001), winner of the *Evening Standard* Charles Wintour Award for Most Promising Playwright; and *Sing Yer Heart Out for the Lads* (National Theatre, 2002). His screenplays include *Offside* and *Bredrens* and his radio plays include *Homeboys*, which was broadcast as part of the Radio 4 First Bite Young Writers' Festival.

117434
Aberdeen College Library

by the same author and also available from Methuen Drama

Starstruck & The No Boys Cricket Club
Lift Off
Clubland
Sing Yer Heart Out for the Lads

ROY WILLIAMS

Plays: 1

The No Boys Cricket Club

Starstruck

Lift Off

introduced by Indhu Rubasingham
with a Foreword by the author

Methuen Drama

METHUEN DRAMA CONTEMPORARY DRAMATISTS

1 3 5 7 9 10 8 6 4 2

This collection first published in Great Britain in 2002 by
Methuen Publishing Limited

Starstruck and *The No Boys Cricket Club* first published by Methuen in 1999
Copyright © Roy Williams 1999, 2002
Lift Off first published by Methuen in 1999
Copyright © Roy Williams 1999, 2002

Foreword copyright © 2002 by Roy Williams
Introduction copyright © 2002 by Indhu Rubasingham

Roy Williams has asserted his rights under the Copyright, Designs
and Patents Act, 1988, to be identified as the author of this work

A CIP catalogue record for this book is available from the British Library

ISBN 0 413 77209 8

Typeset by SX Composing DTP, Rayleigh, Essex
Printed and bound in Great Britain
by Cox & Wyman Ltd, Reading, Berkshire

Caution

All rights in these plays are strictly reserved and application
for performances etc. should be made to: Alan Brodie Representation,
211 Piccadilly, London W1V 9LD.
No performance may be given unless a licence has been obtained.

This book is sold subject to the condition that it shall not, by way of trade
or otherwise, be lent, resold, hired out, or otherwise circulated in any form
of binding or cover other than that in which it is published and without a
similar condition, including this condition, being imposed on the
subsequent purchaser.

ABERDEEN COLLEGE
LIBRARY+
TEL: 01224 612138

Contents

MALGUDI (copyright)

Roy Williams:
A Chronology

1996   *Night and Day* (Theatre Venture tour)
        The No Boys Cricket Club (Theatre Royal, Stratford
        East). Nominated for the TAPS Writer of the Year
        award 1996 and Writers' Guild Best New Writer
        award 1996.
        Josie's Boys (Red Ladder Theatre Co.)
        Homeboys. Broadcast as part of the BBC Radio 4
        First Bite Young Writers' Festival

1998   *Starstruck* (Tricycle Theatre, London). Received the
        first Alfred Fagon Award, the 31st John Whiting
        Award and the EMMA Award 1999.
        Lift Off (Royal Court at the Ambassadors). Joint
        winner of the George Devine Award 2000.
        Souls (Theatre Centre tour)

1999   *Local* Boy (Hampstead Theatre)
        The Gift (Birmingham Repertory Theatre,
        transferred to Tricycle Theatre)

2000   *Clubland* (Royal Court Theatre Upstairs). Won the
        Evening Standard Charles Wintour Award for Most
        Promising Playwright.

2002   *Sing Yer Heart Out for the Lads* (National Theatre,
        Lyttelton Loft).
        Writer in Residence, Royal Court Theatre
        Offside (BBC Television)
        Bredrens (BBC Television)

In development   *Trekkers* (Royal National Theatre Studio)
                  Tell Tale (BBC Television Education)

Foreword

I was a hopeless academic at school. Anything that required me to use my imagination like English or Art, I was good at, but in practical subjects like Maths, Geography – the important stuff – I was useless. I was really falling behind and it got so bad that my family arranged for me to have a private tutor who I would go and see every Saturday. It was either that or getting packed off to stay with relatives in Jamaica and attend school there. My tutor was a man named Don Kinch, who as well as being a teacher was an actor, writer and director with a black theatre company called, at that time, Staunch Poets and Players. Every now and then, instead of our usual Saturday lesson, Don would go and work with his actors on their latest production and I would tag along.

I didn't mind, anything that would get me away from doing my Maths homework was fine with me. So there I was, in this little rehearsal room just off Ladbroke Grove, under the Westway, watching these actors at work. Now, apart from the odd panto visit that I would go to, along with the rest of my school, seeing Don's company was my first real experience of live theatre. I was hooked. Seeing actors perform on stage had a real effect on me. At the time, I knew very little about theatre, except that it was a place that a lot of white people went to, to watch a lot of other white people running about in tights, talking in a funny language that was written by this other white bloke called Shakespeare.

Thank you, Don, for changing that view of mine. I would also like to thank Barrie Keeffe and Nigel Williams for being such good playwrights. When I first read *Class Enemy* and then *Barbarians*, I was totally struck by the fact that these were plays, performed in the theatre, about people I knew, and the world I lived in. I was Snatch in *Class Enemy*, I was Louis in *Barbarians*, and all the other characters were my mates. I realised that theatre wasn't all Shakespeare. It could also be about my life's experiences, my own take on the world. The rest of my school years are a blur, I couldn't wait to get out. I still liked writing, but I never took it seriously. I just didn't believe I could ever be a writer, let alone be paid for it.

So, like most teenagers, I just drifted around for a few years. I worked in McDonalds, Safeways and warehouses. I never stayed longer than a couple of months in any of those jobs. Either I quit, because I was bored, or I was sacked, for the same reason. In 1985, I did a Performing Arts course at Kingsway College – it seemed like a laugh, it was something to do and I was good at it, so I decided to stick with acting for a while. In 1986, I joined the Cockpit Youth Theare. We would meet every Wednesday evening in the rehearsal room upstairs. In that room, we would devise, write, act and direct all of our own work. It was great. During that time, I was offered my first professional acting job, with Theatre Centre, the longest-running theatre company for young people. I was now a 'proper' actor, and I had the Equity card to prove it. I never went to drama school to study acting, so I felt it was important to learn whatever I could, study my craft at Theatre Centre. I stayed with the company for eighteen months. I did four shows and school tours.

During my time at Theatre Centre, I worked with great writers such as Philip Osment, Noel Greig and Lin Coghlan. Watching them work, hearing them talk about their plays, re-ignited my own love for writing. Noel Greig was the company's resident writer at the time and he ran an evening writers' workshop. I asked if I could join, and after a few meetings, I sat down in front of a tattered old typewriter that my mum lent me, and started to write my very first play. It was called *Luke for Gary*, and it was based on a scene that me and my mate Michael Lowe improvised for a show that we appeared in together at the Cockpit Youth Theatre, called *Fists & Fingernails*. In a nutshell, the piece was about two schoolboys, best mates, whose friendship is threatened when everyone assumes they are gay. The boys are reunited at the end, but the piece is left open, without the audience ever knowing for sure if they are gay or not. The last thing I expected was for the play to be picked up by anybody. I was right, although Theatre Centre did give it a reading at the Lillian Bayliss Theatre, where it went down really well. What I was most pleased about was that after all these years of talking about it, I had finally put pen to paper. My time at

Theatre Centre had come to an end. I was now officially a new member of the ever-growing 'resting' actors club. I spent another two years sitting on my arse with no money, waiting for the phone to ring. It didn't.

Luke for Gary was sitting in the bottom drawer somewhere, gathering dust. Whilst resting, I worked at stage door at the Royalty Theatre in London's West End. Eight years had passed since I had left school, and it was there, sitting in that cold stage-door office, that I decided to take my writing seriously. So, one day, I was reading the *Stage*, looking for acting work, when I came across an ad for a writers' course at Rose Bruford College. I decided to apply. Two weeks later, I was offered an interview. I was asked to bring a portfolio of my work. All I had was *Luke for Gary*. I took it out of my drawer, blew the dust off it, and took it with me on my long train journey to Sidcup. I did the interview and in two months I was back at college. Before I knew it, three years had whizzed by. I came out with a First Class Honours degree in Writing and a second play to my name, which was *The No Boys Cricket Club*, the first play in this volume. Part of our degree was to write a full-length stage play. One of my tutors at college, Gilly Fraser, suggested I should send this play out to as many new writing companies as possible.

So, I did. First on my list were the Royal Court, Hampstead Theatre, and Theatre Royal Stratford East. I spent what was left of my grant money on photocopying the scripts, popped them into A4-sized brown envelopes and posted them. I would have sent it to a few more theatres if I had had any more money. Within two months of graduating from Rose Bruford, a radio play which I had written while I was there, entitled *Homeboys*, was commissioned by the BBC for their Young Writers festival, and by then, I had received phone calls from the three companies I had sent the play to. I couldn't believe it – talk about a reaction. I guessed I was good at this writing lark after all. Theatre Royal Stratford East were the ones who ended up producing my stage play, but I had also received commissions to write for the Royal Court and Hampstead. *No Boys* was loosely based on my mother's experiences growing up in Jamaica and living here. The reviews were good, the

Stratford East audience, which are unlike any other, loved it, and I earned a Writers Guild nomination for my trouble. Not a bad way to start my writing career.

The play came out around the time when there seemed to be a new generation of playwrights coming through. David Eldridge, Judy Upton, Rebecca Prichard, Martin McDonagh, Ayub-Khan Din, to name a few. I was glad that my name was included alongside them in several newspapers. It was two and a half years before my next play, *Starstruck*, would be produced, which gave me time to decide what I wanted to write about. They say the second play is always the hardest one to write. *No Boys* focused on a woman leaving Jamaica for England, so for *Starstruck*, I thought it would be interesting to write about a family who didn't leave home but stayed in Jamaica. The piece was commissioned by Stratford East, but found itself performed at The Tricycle Theate in Kilburn in the end, due to Stratford East being rebuilt. Good reviews followed a lovely response from the audience, and I picked up three writing awards for it: the Alfred Fagon Award, the John Whiting Award and an EMMA.

Next up was *Lift Off* for the Royal Court Theatre. I guess you can call it my first 'London' play. I live in Notting Hill (the real Notting Hill, not the one you may have seen in that film). It is arguably the most multicultural part of London, it has always has been. Now, before the likes of Ali G came along, I used to see white kids all around Ladbroke Grove, talking and acting like the black kids. They were not being rude or offensive, they were absolutely genuine, reacting and responding to the world they were living in. I knew there was a play there. The play also won me my fourth award. The George Devine, which I shared with Gary Mitchell.

To say I am overwhelmed by the way my career has been going is an understatement. I can still remember that day, in the summer of 1995, walking down Ladbroke Grove carrying three copies of my play and putting them in the post box. The most I was hoping for from the theatres I had sent them to was 'polite' letters saying how much they liked my play, but it needs work, blah, blah . . . and wishing me good luck in the future. Instead, I got three offers of work. Now, seven years later, I have had two plays performed at the Royal Court, one at the Royal National Theatre, one at the Tricycle, one at Hampstead, one at Birmingham Rep, one at Stratford East, two plays for radio, and one half-hour drama for BBC Television. Even now it still seems hard to believe I have done all that.

People often ask me how I 'churn' scripts out so fast, which I find is a bit of a crude way of describing how I write. It is not a question of 'churning'. Writing any script is bloody tough and each one becomes harder and harder. I just love hard work, I love writing and all the things that come with it, research, interviews, etc. I love it so much that I can easily go through days, sometimes weeks, when I do nothing but write and sleep, every minute of every day. My favourite time to write is in the mornings. I usually get up between five and six and work up until about noon.

I have a short break in the afternoon, then I go back to the computer, and I finish whenever I feel like it. Even when I am not at my computer, I am always thinking about my work, letting it run through my head, twenty-four hours a day, only putting pen to paper (I write everything longhand first) when I believe I have something figured out. Am I mad? Perhaps, but then I'm a writer. Having said that, I have been trying, recently, not to push myself so hard. Not because I love writing any less, but because I think it is important for anyone to look up once in a while, see what's going on in the world, making sure you are not missing out on anything else.

I have been often asked if I mind being called a 'black' playwright, or do I address myself as one? The fact is, I am a playwright, full stop: nothing more, nothing less. I don't write because I am black, I write because I am a writer. I can't be anything else and I don't want to be anything else. I don't care what anyone calls me. 'Black' playwright, 'coloured' play-wright, 'brown' playwright, whatever – just as long as they don't miss out the word playwright. Any time I spend worrying about what people are calling me is time wasted.

Thanks to my best pals, Lincoln (if I hadn't taken your advice, I wouldn't be writing this now), Juliet, Anna, Aslie, Alan, Michael Lowe, Rob, Ruth, Mark Donovan, Grant,

Darren, Maggie, Nancy, Paul, Mel and, of course, Indhu, for all your love and support. Special thanks go to my two oldest buddies, Riz and Stephen, for never once taking the mick, and for all those drinks and meals you bought me when I was skint. To my family: Mum, Mark, Karen and Wally, whom I love so much and never say it enough. To all the people who helped me write these plays, and with my career so far, Paul Everitt, Dominic Tickell, Graham Whybrow, Stephen Daldry, Ian Rickson, Jack Bradley, Stephen Wakelam, Philip Hedley, Nicolas Kent, Stephen Jeffreys, Ultz, Gilly Fraser, John Scotney, David Clough, Roger Smith, Tony Coult, Ben Jancovich, Donna Franceschild, all the casts and crew of these three plays, and of course my brilliant agent Alan Brodie and everyone else at ABR, cheers.

I would also like to thank Winsome Pinnock, Mustapha Matura, Bonnie Greer, Caryl Philips, Alfred Fagon, Biyi Bandele, August Wilson, Nigel Williams, Lorraine Hansberry, Arthur Miller, Noel Greig, Lin Coghlan, Philip Osment, and Barrie Keefe, for all of the wonderful work that inspired me to follow you. Love and hugs to anyone else I have forgotten to mention. And last but not least, to Luke and Gary for starting it all. Thank you, boys.

Roy Williams
March 2002

Introduction

In September 1995, the Theatre Royal, Stratford East sent me a new play to read. It was called *The No Boys Cricket Club* by Roy Williams, which he had written in his final year at Rose Bruford College. I was immediately drawn to the script and the story told. A reading was organised at Stratford East, where I first met Roy. I think the shock to most people, including myself, was that this play which focused so sensitively on the lives of two middle-aged women was written by a young man (and in those days a shy young man!).

The play followed the lives of two middle-aged West Indian women living in London. Their lives are full of disappointment and disillusion. They hark back to a time when they were filled with excitement and hope about their future. For them, this was when, as teenagers in Kingston, Jamaica, they formed a No Boys Cricket Club. Dramatically, the opportunity arises for them in present-day London to revisit their youth and meet their younger selves. The theatrical potential of this piece was immediately apparent; to read a first play that had a magical quality but was based on very real characters was thrilling. A remembered world was juxtaposed with the grittier present-day London, so that two characters, one younger and the other much older, could meet on stage. The game of cricket was being used as a metaphor for dreams, strength and the rediscovery of self.

The No Boys Cricket Club had not been commissioned, so when Stratford East programmed it for the following year, this was a huge achievement. Not only did it demonstrate Roy's talent and ability, but also, equally importantly, the theatre's commitment and courage in programming an unknown writer almost immediately.

In May 1996, I directed *No Boys Cricket Club* at Stratford East for a four-week run. The play follows the character of Abi, a sixty-year-old Jamaican woman living in the East End, trying to hold her family together. Her dead husband was someone she never loved; her son is a drug-pusher who is now back living at home. Her daughter is getting into trouble with gangs and just as life gets even worse, we see Abi literally escape into the past with her best friend, Masie.

In the production at Stratford East, you could hear gasps from the audience when the stage changed for the first time from contemporary, grey London to the magical beach in Jamaica. As one audience member told the designer, 'Thank you, you took me back home!'

Roy poignantly explores the possibility of what it would be like to meet your younger self. What would you tell her? What would you try to do to change the future? But instead of the older Abi advising the young Abi in this play, it is the other way around.

> **Young Abi** You did it, didn't you, you gave up, that's why you're here . . . You should have held on. So wat are you then. Not a nurse I take it. Come on someone's cleaner, summin' like that . . . You see me? This Abigail Sanford would never give up. I know who I am, I don't know you. I hate you.

Through this confrontation, you see the young Abi being the teacher. In the course of the act, she makes the older Abi face up to the reality of her own life.

What Roy shows us at the end is that Abi now has more hope and an ability to stand up for herself. But even if things can change, it is at a price. Roy doesn't give us a easy ending, as Abi's daughter Danni points out: 'You'll give up. You always do.'

In *No Boys' Cricket Club* we see the beginnings of themes Roy explores more fully in later plays. His obvious talent for dialogue is there, particularly the contemporary urban sounds in the younger generation of this play, best demonstrated through Faye, the neighbour. There's also his interest in exploring taboos, in challenging his audience, never unnecessarily, but because extraordinary things always happen in ordinary circumstances. There is an incident in the play where Michael, the son, hits his mother, albeit by accident. There was a strong resistance from the actors to this moment. They insisted that this would never happen in a Jamaican household and the audience were always shocked – an audible gasp, murmurs of disapproval followed the hit. However, Roy felt this aspect of life should be exposed and as he himself said, 'I know it happens. I'm not saying it's a common occurrence but I know it happens.'

What makes Roy's plays entertaining is that comedy is juxtaposed with the grittier truth. The contradictions are what make intolerable characters likeable. He takes audiences out of their comfortable middle-class assumptions and tells us not to simply observe but forces us to empathise. This is something that he continues to develop throughout his writing.

Starstruck was Roy's next play to be produced. When I was asked to direct a play at the Tricycle Theatre, I suggested *Starstruck*, as Roy and I had developed a complementary way of working together which was very satisfying and creative. It was produced in the autumn of 1998. The characters in this play are more complex, which was perhaps in part to do with the process of collaboration with actors that Roy had experienced during rehearsals for *No Boys Cricket Club*; they had asked him difficult questions about the characters and their journeys, and this was reflected in the writing of his next play. This play was set in the seventies in Jamaica. The magical element is still there in *Starstruck*, represented by the off-stage 'dream world' of the filming of a Stewart Granger movie on the island.

The most complex character in the play is Hope, a middle-aged woman. Even though she is having an affair with her nephew while her husband, Gravel, has been ill, the audience can't help but empathise with her predicament at the end because after Gravel's death and her son's rejection she is desolate. Hope is not a victim or vixen, but a woman who was born at the wrong time. She aspired to go to England, and dreamed of falling madly in love and living happily ever after, but instead was left on her own in Kingston, pregnant. She is a dissatisfied woman who lives out her hopes and dreams through her son, Dennis.

Dennis wants to be a movie star; he thinks he will achieve his dream, especially when he gets a bit part on the Stewart Granger film. He, too, dreams of going to London, to RADA. However, his girlfriend, Pammy, wants him to settle down in Kingston. We see life repeating itself when he gets Pammy pregnant and is faced with a dilemma. Gravel wants Dennis to face up to his responsibility as a father, but Hope wants Dennis to follow his own dreams and go to London.

The theme of this play is disappointed dreams. Roy asks us whether in growing older, we must sacrifice our youthful dreams. Through the marriage of Gravel and Hope, Roy pits aspirations against responsibility; neither seems a perfect option. Hope yearns for her lost love, Gravel's brother, and the promise of adventures overseas. She says, 'I wan' feel love dat mek me live a whole lifetime's-worth in one night!' She is the most poetic of all the characters, even though she is forcing her dreams on to her son and grabbing at life without a thought of the consequences. Her yearnings are what we understand – her unrequited love. Her life is overburdened with responsibility for her, and we sympathise with that. Gravel on the other hand is the opposite side of the coin and takes his responsibilities to the extreme. He married his brother's jilted, pregnant girlfriend in order to provide for her and her child, Dennis. Although he has always loved Hope, he knows she can never love him like she loved his brother. It is a knowledge he suffers from and he constantly lives in that shadow.

Hope is forever indebted to Gravel. Both are dissatisfied and unhappy as neither is living the lives they wanted – Gravel's choices will eventually kill him. The future is in Dennis. Will Dennis repeat his parents' patterns? Can he break the cycle? Through the revelations of the play, he discovers that Gravel is not his real father and his mother falls from her pedestal, so finally he decides to stay on the island and face his duties. But in the final moment of the play we see him quoting Shakespeare as he paints a sign, which reads 'Gravel & Son'. In this moment we know that his dreams of acting have not vanished. The sign is clearly a lie, as he is not Gravel's son. By this action, Roy shows that Dennis may be repeating both Gravel's and Hope's mistakes, by living a lie.

With both *No Boys Cricket Club* and *Starstruck*, Roy questions the reality of the immigration experience in this country. He shows how for many of our parents' generation the reality of Britain was not what they had hoped for. Although Dennis doesn't come to England, the audience will know that it was impossible for a black actor to become a film star in Britain in the early seventies. Yet we also know that the fact he stays means that he will remain frustrated. Similarly with *No Boys*, Young Abi dreams of becoming a nurse and coming to England to achieve this, but in reality we see that Abi is disappointed in Britain and her spirit is depleted.

Roy's melancholic view of the past is reflected in his feelings about multicultural Britain today. How inclusive and equal is our society?

The *No Boys Cricket Club* and *Starstruck* deal with the themes of the past, our parents' generation and the sense of failed dreams. The landscape of Britain has changed radically within a couple of generations and those of us with parents who emigrated here now have a completely different experience of Britain. Our parents were foreigners. We are not. Their stories were not necessarily encouraged thirty years ago. However, we need their stories to tell us how we got here, to this exact point. Both these plays deal with the Dick Whittington myth – the lesson that the streets are not always paved with gold. Roy pays homage to his heritage by telling the stories that our parents were not able to tell. Through them, he is also exploring the ambivalence of the society that his generation has inherited, the so-called multicultural one that we live in now. In his plays he neither condones nor condemns the choices that his parents' generation made.

It would be simple to put Roy's plays into a category of 'black' plays but to do that would be to do his work an injustice. These stories are a microcosm of the journey we *all* make, when the dreams of our youth crumble to the point where they completely disappear – the growing pains of life. These are universal stories told through a specific context. Roy's vision gives us not only a cultural and racial insight but also lends itself to a unique theatricality which develops through cultural contrast. For example, in *No Boys Cricket Club*, it is fascinating to see the contrast between contemporary London and Jamaica in the fifties.

After Starstruck, Roy's first production at the Royal Court Theatre materialised. I directed *Lift Off* at the Royal Court in

February 1999. The themes he explores here are those that concern the urban scene in London. He examines the very British context, specifically contemporary London and its multiracial identity.

Lift Off follows the relationship between Mal and Tone, two young men, black and white friends respectively, in west London. In this play Roy investigates the current fashion for 'being black' and what the reality of this actually means. Mal is the cool black guy on the estate. All the girls fancy him and Tone desperately wants to be like him. So Tone speaks 'black', tries to dress 'black', but that's where the likeness ends.

Roy is examining friendship and identity in this play. We see Mal and Tone when they were younger, starting secondary school, meeting Rich, a young black kid, in the playground. Rich doesn't act 'black' enough. The young Mal thinks that if you're black you have to be cool, you have to be hard:

Young Mal   It's the only way to be, man. Show yer temper a bit more, prove yer hard. Yu hear wat I said? . . . He ain't black. Fuck knows wat he is.

Roy examines this definition and presents us with a pessimistic view. What happens if you are black, but are neither cool nor hard, where does this leave you? Rich, who doesn't conform to this stereotype, ends up committing suicide. This event haunts Mal throughout his life. The play shows how little space there is in urban London to genuinely define and explore your identity without coming up against the constraints of racial stereotypes, either positive or negative. The dialogue is fast and immediately recognisable, as Roy has a fantastic ear for urban language and rhythms.

His language not only has great theatricality, but immense political resonance. Seeing a white guy on stage speaking 'black' is very powerful in itself. This demonstrates Tone's desperation to be like Mal and his own absence of identity. However, in the play this friendship is betrayed by Mal sleeping with Tone's under-age sister, Carol, and getting her pregnant. Worse still, Mal apparently does not care and is flippant and derogatory about her. Tone is outraged and calls

Mal a 'Nigger . . . Black bastard' in a heated confrontation, impulsively. This is an uncomfortable moment in the audience. Mal is not an innocent in this situation. We see the repercussions and injury his actions have caused. Yet does this justify racist insults? Mal in turn has his own anger. He has leukaemia. There are not enough black people on the register donating blood, so what is the point of being cool according to the media and popular culture when the very thing that makes you cool could cause your death?

Mal puts the harsh reality of the choices he faces to Tone:

Yes! Thass wat I am, and niggers don't care Tone, it's not in us. I mean we'd rather stuff our faces wid fried chicken, go out and teif, fuck whoever we like, than give blood to one of our own who badly needs it – who could die if he don't get it.

The play shows that whatever the state of the friendship, race is an issue that has to be negotiated even amongst the closest friends. No matter how much you might want to identify with another culture, it is only ever a perception of being black and not the reality. Roy plays with all the stereotypical images that are presented to us and makes them into contradictory and complex characters.

He forces an audience to explore what it means to be British and he doesn't make it pleasant. His use of language is always refreshing, but absolutely real. What runs through all his plays are the repercussions of the past in the present. There is a deep sense of morality in his plays, a world view which shows that you have to face up to your actions at some point and the sins of the father being passed down. Yet no matter how dark and unsavoury his characters are, he makes them vulnerable, by showing that they too are constrained and defined by society's pressures and perceptions.

Roy is one of the most prolific playwrights to have emerged in the late nineties. He has had a remarkable amount of work produced in a short period of time. This is not just due to his own industrious nature but primarily because he creates contemporary characters familiar to so many people in a way that has never been done before in theatre. His plays capture a world that is immediately recognisable but very rarely seen on stage. In November 2001, I was delighted to be at the *Evening Standard* awards with Roy, where he was given the Most Promising Playwright award for *Clubland*, which I directed at the Royal Court. It was a great moment to see him receive the recognition he deserves.

Indhu Rubasingham
March 2002

The No Boys Cricket Club

The No Boys Cricket Club was first performed at the Theatre Royal, Stratford East, London, on 24 May 1996. The cast was as follows:

Abi	Donna Croll
Masie	Anni Domingo
Danni	Michele Joseph
Michael	Steve Toussaint
Faye	Nina Conti
Young Abi	Ashley Miller
Young Masie	Sharon Duncan Brewster
Ferdy Watson	Jason Rose
Jenny	Natasha Gordon
Shirley	Karlene Saunders
Cita	Trixie Munyama

Reece, Miss Devereaux and the Clanton Street Boys were played by members of the cast.

Directed by Indhu Rubasingham
Designed by Rosa Maggiora
Lighting by Chris Davey

Characters

Abi, 53
Danni, 19, Abi's daughter
Michael, 26, Abi's son
Faye, 21
Masie, 53
Ferdy, Masie's husband
Young Abi
Young Masie
Jenny ⎫
Shirley ⎬ The No Boys Cricket Club
Cita ⎭
Reece, Faye's boyfriend
Miss Devereaux
The Clanton Street Boys

The play is set in the garden of a council house in present-day London and in Kingston Town, Jamaica, 1958.

Act One

Scene One

Abi *enters from the house, carrying a bag of washing. She hangs the clothes on the washing line, she looks up when she hears voices somewhere. Voices of young girls playing cricket. She looks around and can see something.*

Abi   Jenny Vincent, no, man, no.

Shirley (*offstage*)   You're out, out . . .

Jenny (*offstage*)   Oh shut up, ya breath come like frog . . .

Shirley (*offstage*)   Out, out out!

Abi   Oh yeah, go on girl, go on.

Sound of a cricket ball being hit. **Abi** *laughs out.*

Cita (*offstage*)   Run na girl . . .

All the girls cheer. They call out the name **Abi**.

Abi (*to audience*)   That game had me buzzing like some bee for the whole week. It was sunny, we reserved the field two weeks in advance and I was on serious form. Me, Abigail Rosemary Sandford.

Sound of another ball being whacked.

Straight up, you see it, boom! We were playing class 2C, throughout the week during schoolbreaks, and we were beating the pants off them. They could only get twelve runs out of us when they were up. Today was our last day, and soon we go put them out of misery forever, soon.

A school bell is rung. The girls cheer.

Young Masie (*offstage*)   Abi girl you were on fire!

Young Abi (*offstage*)   Y' think so Masie?

Young Masie (*offstage*)   Oh stop it, you know so. You country girls are summin else. I'm still waiting for that last ball to come down.

Young Abi (*offstage*)   Must be in Frankfield by now.

Young Masie (*offstage*)   Na, Guyana.

Young Abi (*offstage*)   Florida!

Miss Devereaux (*offstage*)   Masie Williams, Abigail Sandford, would you girls mind gracing me with your presence in the classroom?

Young Abi/Young Masie (*offstage*)   Coming Miss Devereaux.

Abi (*laughs. Then stares at something.*)   Yes?

The voices fade away as loud popular music comes blaring out of the house. **Abi** *is slightly bewildered, but comes to.*

(*Yelling.*) Michael, will you turn the music down na man, Michael!

The music is turned down a bit. **Abi** *returns to her washing, but her peace is shortlived as she now hears yelling from the next-door garden.*

Faye (*offstage*)   You lying bastard, you ain't going anywhere.

Reece (*offstage*)   I've had enough of your shit!

Abi (*to herself*)   Now they're gonna start up.

Faye (*offstage*)   You ain't going.

Abi   Shut up over there. (*To herself.*) Every blasted day!

Michael *pops his head out from one of the bedroom windows.*

Michael (*offstage*)   Mum, wat you yelling for, I've turned it down, ain't I?

Abi   Not you, them.

Michael (*offstage*)   They're at it again?

Abi   Where's Dannielle?

Michael (*offstage*)   In the bloody bathroom still, tell her to come out now Mum.

Abi   Do not swear Michael.

Michael   Just tell her, I gotta go out soon.

Abi   Keep her inside for me, I don't want her seeing this.

Michael   What they're yelling about now?

Abi   Michael if you want to talk to me, come out here please.

Michael   You come in here.

Abi   You wan' to eat in this house?

The neighbours are still at it.

Shut up!

Reece (*offstage*)   You dumb bitch, now you're bothering the neighbours.

Faye (*offstage*)   I don't care about her.

Abi   What she say?

Reece (*offstage*)   Gimme back my keys Faye.

Faye (*offstage*)   So go get them.

The door opens, a set of keys are tossed out.

Abi   But Jesus Christ.

Reece (*offstage*)   You're gonna go right out and get them back.

Faye (*offstage*)   You're the one who wants to go out with that slag.

Reece (*offstage*)   There's only one slag I know, an' I'm looking at her.

Abi   Damn right.

Faye (*offstage*)   You bastard . . .

Michael (*offstage*)   Go get my keys!

Faye (*offstage*)   Go screw!

Sound of the girl being slapped. **Faye** *comes out, picks up the keys, and walks back in, coldly acknowledging* **Abi**.

Faye   Yes?

Faye *goes back in.*

Abi   About she don't care what I think, we'll soon see when the council drag her arse out, she'll care plenty then, plenty.

Michael *comes out bare-chested.*

Michael   Mum, who are you talking to?

Abi (*slightly embarrassed*)   Don't stand out like that in the cold Michael, you catch cold. What do you want?

Michael (*delves into the basket, takes out some socks*)   That and that.

Abi   They're not dry yet.

Michael   They'll be alright, once over with an iron.

Abi   You mean to say you've got no clean socks in your room?

Michael   No.

Abi   Boy have no shame. Where you going in such a hurry?

Michael   Out.

Abi   Out where?

Michael   Out there, I don't ask you about your business Mum.

Abi   What business is that, apart from cleaning up after you pikne?

Michael   'Lord nobody don't love me!'

Abi   Only people that give me the time of day is gas, electric an' telephone. You see the bill?

Michael   You'll get my share, but there is Danni as well you know.

Abi   She's studying.

Michael   She's a pain. She ain't getting her room back.

Abi   Oh not this again.

Michael   It was mine to begin with, she shouldn't have leaped in there in the first place.

Abi   Alright, alright, but I still want money from you.

Michael   Yeah soon Mum, I'm skint right now.

Abi   Skint? Of course you're skint, with your 80-pound trainers.

Michael   They don't cost 80 quid Mum.

Abi   Don't take me for a fool. I see your friend Gary Warren wid the same pair, he told me how much they cost, 80 pounds. (*Raises her foot.*) You see these, £2.99 from the market, 1984. Spend any of your money on Patrick?

Michael   I was wondering when you were gonna start with that.

Abi   Well have you?

Michael   Leave it Mum.

Abi   Should be ashamed.

Michael   Patrick will get money when I'm good and ready, you'll get money when I'm good and ready. (*Under his breath.*) For fuck's sake . . . (*Goes inside.*)

Abi   Don't swear at me Michael. If your father was alive today he'd . . .

Michael (*cutting off*) . . . give me two good licks in my head!

Michael *comes back out with some letters.*

Michael   There's a letter for you. (*Hands it over.*) I've got two.

Abi   That's nice.

Michael   Do you want the stamps?

Abi   If you like.

Michael   Christ. Here. (*Gives them to her.*)

Abi   Thank you kind sir.

Michael   It's alright.

Abi (*reads the back of her letter*)   But Jesus Christ! Masie Williams, so it's now you decide to write to me girl!

Abi *tears open the letter.*

Michael   Who's Masie?

Abi   Your Aunt Masie.

Michael   Yeah, you want to narrow that down for me?

Abi   Your Aunt Masie from Streatham.

Michael   We ain't got family in Streatham.

Abi   Yes you do.

Michael   Who?

Abi (*irritated*)   Your Aunt Masie.

Michael   Oh man!

Abi   You remember your Uncle Ferdy, her husband, and Claudia, Jeffrey and Vanessa.

Michael   More cousins. Nice. They from Dad's side?

Abi   No!

Michael   Then how is she my aunt?

Abi   We grew up back home.

Michael   Oh home, yeah and so?

Abi   So she is like a sister, she's your elder, you treat her with respect.

Michael   I ain't even met her.

Abi   Oh go about your business and let me read my letter.

A loud banging on a door is heard from inside.

Danni (*offstage*)   Mum!

Abi   Lord Jesus, once, just once, can I have some peace in my own home?

Michael   Must be Danni, Mum.

Abi   Dannielle stop your noise. What is wrong with that girl?

Michael   Me locking her in the bathroom might have summin to do with it.

Abi   Why did you do that?

Michael   You told me to!

Abi   Boy how old are you, don't answer that. Go and open the door.

Michael *curses as he goes back in.* **Abi** *tries to get back to her letter but is disturbed yet again when* **Faye** *comes out carrying a stack of records; she tosses them on to the floor.* **Abi** *looks up, they glare at each other.*

Faye   Yes!

Abi *kisses her teeth.*

Danni (*offstage*)   Wass the bloody matter with you?

Michael (*offstage*)   Mum told me to do it.

Danni (*offstage*)   Where is she?

Abi *stops reading. She folds the letter and waits for her daughter* **Danni** *who enters wearing a bathrobe.*

Danni　Mum what you playing at, why you telling him to lock me in the bathroom?

Abi　I didn't . . .

At this point, **Faye** *comes out again, carrying more records. She dumps them with the others.*

Danni　Faye, Faye?

Abi　Don't go over there. Dannielle Carter.

Danni *climbs over.*

Abi　I see, this is what you do when I tell you not to do things.

Danni　He hit her again, why didn't you say?

Abi　But what's it got to do with you?

Faye *comes out,* **Danni** *blocks her path.*

Danni　Faye what's this all about?

Faye　I don't want a single thing in here belonging to that bastard, I don't want nothing.

Danni　What's he done? Faye!

Faye　Jackie Willis come tell me, to my face right, that she saw Reece and some young slag at a rave together, an' they weren't just chatting.

Danni　You know what Jackie's like.

Faye　I know what Reece is like as well.

Danni　You don't know that.

Faye　You an expert on men or summin?

Abi　Hey, young lady, she is the only friend you have.

Danni　Mum for chrissake.

Abi (*to* **Danni**)　When are you going to wake up to her child? Look I got a letter from your Aunt Masie.

Danni Triffic. Why don't you sit down with it and be quiet Mum.

Abi Don't talk to me like I'm some fool girl.

Faye Last time he does that to me.

Danni You've said that before.

Faye I've never thrown out his records before.

Danni He'll slap you around again.

Faye You reckon? (*Goes back in.*)

Danni Faye?

Faye *comes back carrying a knife.*

Danni Fuck.

Faye Thass right, he ain't gonna hit me no more.

Danni As soon as you've sobered up, he'll grab it off ya.

Faye Well what else can I do, Miss Know-all?

Danni Leave him.

Faye And go where?

Abi She's not coming here.

Faye Did I ask?

Danni Mum stay out of it.

Abi Your Aunt Masie has a daughter, Claudia, 19 years old, four 'A' levels, (*in* **Faye***'s direction*) 'A' levels!

Faye Whoopee fuckin' do!

Abi Dannielle, what did she just say to me?

Danni Nothing.

Abi She's a smart young lady, got a baby girl.

Faye Can't be that smart then.

Danni   Mum is there any point to this?

Abi   I'm just telling you about your Aunt Masie's children.

Danni   I ain't got a Aunt Masie.

Faye *grunts in laughter.*

Faye   Your Mum's gone, big time.

Danni   Rub it in, why don't ya. Come on Faye.

Faye *hands over the knife.* **Abi** *is no longer listening to them. She is shaken by something she has read.*

Faye   I fuckin' hate him Danni, I deserve better than this.

Danni   I know.

Faye   Mum won't even come round to see us because of him. Now she wants me to move back in with them, no bloody way!

Danni   She's alright half the time.

Faye   You an expert on mothers now?

Danni   No.

Faye   I don't know how you can stand living with yours. Look at her, look. You want to grow up to be like that?

Danni   Not so loud.

Danni *watches her mother.*

Faye   No wonder Shanelle is running you down.

Danni   Alright Faye!

Faye   You know what she's saying, about your family, Michael. That you're all dealing in it. (*Laughs.*) Ain't true is it?

Danni   No it bloody ain't!

Faye's *front door is slammed.*

Faye   That's him out for the night. (*Sound of a baby crying.*)
Now he has to fuckin' start. (*Shouting.*) I'm coming alright! So
what are you going to do about Shanelle?

Danni   I'll see to it.

Faye   Nice one, give her a kick in the head for me.

Faye *goes back in,* **Danni** *climbs back over.*

Danni   You made me look bad Mum, don't you ever stop,
Mum?

Abi   I'm sorry what did you say?

Danni   Nuttin forget it.

Danni *goes back in, but not before* **Michael** *passes her and taps
her on the head.*

Danni   Move!

Michael   Or what! Mum, do this tie for me, one of your
special knots nice and loose yeah Mum, come on, quick
time.

Abi   Yes, yes, alright.

Michael   You alright? Mum are you alri . . .

Abi   Yes I'm fine. So where are you off to?

Michael   Just out. No, that's too tight, do it again.

Abi   Out with your friends, wasting time on foolishness,
should be ashamed.

Michael   Now that's too loose, come on Mum.

Abi   I'm trying.

Michael   Try harder.

Abi   What kind of tie is this? (*Reading.*) Guchy, gucky,
what?

Michael   Gucci.

Abi   Wasting your money, ain't seen my grandson in months.

Michael   Will you come off that please?

Abi   A Gucci tie instead of Patrick, you want to get your priorities straight.

Michael   The bloody tie Mum.

Abi *tightens it, almost choking* **Michael**.

Abi   You should treasure every moment to be with him, how long do you think that lasts, how long?

Michael (*pushing her away*)   Forget the tie, I'll do it myself. Wass the matter wid you?

Abi   Your Aunt Masie. Her boy Jeffrey, he's gone.

Michael   Gone where?

Abi   He's dead, Jeffrey's dead.

Abi *begins to sob.*

Michael   Oh man, oh chriss Mum, juss hang on. (*Calling.*) Oi ugly, ugly!

Danni   I got a name shithead.

Michael   Never mind your name, go make some tea quick time.

Danni   You got hands.

Michael   It's for Mum.

Abi   No I don't . . .

Danni   She's got hands.

Michael   Put the kettle on now!

Danni   Go get one of your girlfriends pregnant!

Michael   You fuckin' little . . .

Abi   Michael stop your swearing.

Michael   Tea on its way Mum, right Danni!

Abi   I don't want any blasted tea.

Michael   Yeah but I just . . . alright.

Abi   I have to go, right now . . . Masie needs me, I have to go.

Michael   Yeah, course.

Danni   Tea will soon be ready Mum, oh yeah ignore me why don't you.

Danni *enters, she sees her brother.*

Danni   What's up with Mum?

Michael   Bad news from Aunt Masie.

Danni (*irritated*)   Who's Aunt Masie?

Michael   Fucked if I know.

Scene Two

The cricket pitch, Kingston. **Abi** *is watching* **Young Masie** *getting ready to bowl.*

Abi   Masie Williams was the captain of our little team and my best friend ever. She never had much. Mother ran off when she was just a baby. So she went from one relative to the other. Everyone thought she'd turn out bad, but she was the fastest bowler I ever saw. Lord could she bowl, Jesus!

As soon as **Young Masie** *bowls, lights fully on cricket field.* **Young Masie** *has just bowled out* **Young Abi**.

Young Masie   You're out, out, out!

Young Abi   Yes alright Masie.

Young Masie   Got to take the highs with the lows Abi.

Young Abi   I know, I'm just glad you're bowling for us.

Young Masie   I'm glad you're glad. But we couldn't do it without you you know.

Young Abi   We are just a little team Masie, summin for fun, after school.

Young Masie   Summin for fun! Listen girl you know what Dedee Jones' brother Smokey have the nerve to say to me the other day?

Young Abi   No but you're going to tell me.

Young Masie   He says him and his boys from Clanton Street can beat us in a game, us! (*Laughs.*)

Young Abi   You didn't challenge him did you?

Young Masie   A few weeks from now.

Young Abi   Oh Masie girl!

Young Masie   Come on we can beat them.

Young Abi   We got exams coming, you said we wouldn't play till the vacations.

Young Masie   We'll start practising this weekend.

Young Abi   No, we can't.

Young Masie   Why not?

Young Abi   Weekends is when Daddy comes back from the country.

Young Masie   And when was the last time you seen him?

Young Abi   He said he would this time. He's bringing me back a present.

Young Masie   He won't.

Young Abi   He will!

Young Masie   We need you.

Young Abi   He needs me. Oh you make it so difficult sometimes. He's my only real family Masie. I shouldn't be wasting time with this foolishness.

Young Masie   That's Miss Tyler talking.

Young Abi   Don't say that woman's name to me.

Young Masie   Miss Tyler, Miss Tyler . . .

Young Abi   Stop it!

Young Masie   I'm right though. Ain't right, things she says to you, ain't right at all.

Young Abi   She was Moma's sister.

Young Masie   Don't excuse her.

Young Abi   She blames me.

Young Masie   Tell her to go to hell.

Young Abi   What!

Young Masie   Yes!! You're Abigail Sandford, and you should do what you want to do, am I right?

Young Abi   Like, play for the team?

Young Masie   Why not?

Young Abi   Yeah you're Abigail Sandford, and you should do what you want, just as long as it's what Masie Williams wants.

Young Masie   Hold on a minute. You're our star player girl, it's truth. You say your daddy loves cricket? Well bring him along, let him watch, but he can't coach us.

Young Abi (*pleading*)   Masie . . .

Young Masie (*pleading*)   Abi . . .

Young Abi   Look, we'll see, but I'm not promising anything.

Young Masie   Thank you darling, you'll never let me down.

Young Abi   Hold on I didn't say for definite . . . (**Young Masie** *starts packing up*.) Wat is it with you girl, you want to rule the world or something?

Young Masie   Good idea.

Young Abi   What's the hurry?

Young Masie   Ferdy Watson was pulling my hair in class today.

Young Abi   And Miss Devereaux put him in a corner, and you kicked him in the arse all the way home, so?

Young Masie   We ran past Miss Stuart, nearly knocked her out of her stool, you know wat they say about her, how she's never wrong about anything. She told me one day me and Ferdy Watson are going get married, have children, can you think of anything more disgusting, Ferdy's kids? Well she is wrong about this, it won't happen girl, you hear me? But you carry on, you wanna end up with Teddy Carter, thass your business.

Young Abi   Teddy Carter g'way!

Young Masie   I saw that sweet he passed you, you country girls think you're so sly.

Young Abi   He wants to join the team.

Young Masie   I hope you said no.

Young Abi   He's good with a bat.

Young Masie   We are not called the No Boys Cricket Club for nothing Abi.

Young Abi   Look I've seen the way those Clanton boys play.

Young Masie   We can beat them.

Young Abi   Why is this so important?

Young Masie   If you coulda seen the way old man Rivers was laughing when he heard about the game, he says if we win, he'll put our picture on the front of the paper.

Young Abi   Front?

Young Masie   Front page!

Young Abi   Don't wish for the impossible Masie.

Young Masie   There's nothing wrong with wishing. We're going places Abi I can feel it and no stupid gang of boys is going to mess this up you hear me?

Scene Three

London, five days later. **Michael** *comes from the alleyway and places bags of drugs under the plantpots.* **Danni** *comes out.*

Danni   What are you up to?

Michael   Get lost.

Danni   You bloody liar.

Michael   Say that again? Y' think I don't know your game, you're lucky I don't bust your head now. I suppose I have to hide these in my room now, you so fuckin' nosey. (*He stashes them in his pocket.*) How do I look?

Danni   Like someone with bags of drugs stuffed in their pocket.

Michael   You're not funny.

Danni   Just walk through quickly.

Michael   She'll spot these a mile off.

Danni   Doubt it. Mum and Aunt Masie are now talking about where to get the best Jamaican patties from – London or Birmingham.

Michael   Na, she can't help herself but ask. I ain't got time for a scene with her.

Danni   Scared.

Michael   Not as scared as you will be.

Danni   I ain't afraid of you Michael.

Michael   No? (*Prodding her.*)

Danni   No!

Michael   How did Mum and Dad ever have such a weakling of a kid.

Danni   Oh don't put yourself down broth.

Michael   There goes your mouth again, you ever wonder why you get into so much trouble?

Danni   I know why.

Michael   Oh let me guess, because of your big bad brother?

Danni   Why can't you piss off? Everyone knows about you Michael. You ain't that clever the only one who don't know nuttin is Mum.

Michael   Well let's do our best to keep it from her. I'm out of here.

Danni   Don't get picked up by the police now?

Michael (*laughs*)   You and your mouth.

Michael *leaves through the alleyway.* **Danni** *sits on the steps leading up to the house. She reads her paper.* **Abi**, *and* **Masie**, *come out. They nearly trip over* **Danni**.

Abi   Oh will you stop with that . . .

Masie   I'm telling you girl . . .

Abi   Dannielle, don't sit there, you tryin' to kill us?

Masie   Those fools they got playing for us don't know nuttin about cricket, letting those stupid white boys beat them. Especially that big ugly one that's always in the papers, with the moustache, whatshisname? You think he coulda bowled out Abigail Sandford, no way! This was you. (*Pretending to bat.*) Pow, and pow another pow!

Abi   Masie shush.

Masie   No, and you went pow!

Abi   Alright.

Danni   Whass all this?

Masie   Whass all this? Child you mean to say you didn't know your mother was a devil wid a bat?

Danni   No.

Masie   She was the best, she go like this, pow and pow!

Abi   Stop your noise.

Masie (*laughs*)   You know it's true.

Abi   Yes!

Danni   You used to play cricket Mum?

Masie   We didn't just play Dannielle, we lived. Wan' to hear about it?

Abi   Not right now Masie.

Masie (*pleading*)   Abi . . .

Abi   No! Where are you going?

Danni   What makes you think I'm going anywhere?

Abi   Your face. I want to talk to you.

Danni   Will it take long?

Abi   As long as it needs to. I saw your friend Shanelle today.

Danni   Did you?

Abi   She says she's looking forward to seeing you.

Danni   Good.

Abi   I don't like that girl, she's got too much to say for herself.

Danni   Great, you don't like Shanelle you don't like Faye.

Abi   What's going on Dannielle?

Masie   Let her go Abi.

Danni   Thank you Aunt Masie.

Abi   Just tell me.

Danni   Mum I'm seeing a friend from college, you'll like her, five 'A' levels and goes to church every Sunday, can I go?

Abi   You think I'm stupid?

Danni   Why would I think that Mum?

Abi   If it was raining right now but Faye said it was sunny, would you run out arse-naked?

Danni   Can I go?

Abi   I'm trying to help you.

Danni   Yeah right.

Abi   Don't!

Masie   Come on Abi.

Abi   Masie please.

Masie   You remember that time when we went out fishing wid the Brewster boys? All the girls warned us not to go, but we went anyway.

Danni   Later Mum.

Abi   Danni . . .

Masie   We shoulda worn iron bras.

Danni   Mum I'm just . . . (*Realising what* **Masie** *has said.*)
You wat!

Abi   Nothing! (*Ushering her out.*) Just go about your business,
Danni. And don't slam the . . . (*Door is slammed.*) door.

Masie (*feeling* **Abi***'s glare*)   Did I do something wrong?

Abi   There was no need for her to hear a story like that.

Masie   Oh come on, don't you hear wat they say
nowadays? Seen it, heard it, bought the T-shirt. They're
gonna do what they want so let them get on with it.

Abi   You don't mean that.

Masie   Oh yes I do. When Claudia was thirteen, I caught
her leaving the house with some big red lipstick on her face,
my lipstick, I told her 'Girl you best wipe that off'. Hear wat
she says, 'Oh but Mum, Tina's mum lets her wear make-
up'. (**Abi** *laughs.*) It's true . . .

Abi   . . . 'It isant fair . . .'

Masie   'Tina's mum lets her do whatever she wants . . .'

Abi   Not just mums though. What about the fathers?
Michael would always make me look bad in front of his
daddy.

Masie   That's Jeffrey and Ferdy all over, the tings that
boy would get himself into, just to prove to his daddy how
big and tough he is. They do it anyway, so why bother
yourself. Abi? You're staring at me girl what is it?

Abi   It's strange to hear you talk, like he was still alive.

Masie   I know my boy is dead Abi.

Abi   I'm sorry.

Masie   It's alright.

Abi   Oh Masie, what can I say to make it better huh? (*She takes her hand.*) It's good to see you.

Masie   It's good to be seen. Thanks for coming to the funeral.

Abi   Oh hush.

Masie   You know, even at the reception, his mother still found time to turn up her nose at the food.

Abi   She lost her only grandson.

Masie   No, it goes deeper than that. You know, on my wedding day, I found her in my room, packing my clothes, she had my cricket bat thrown in the dustbin, dustbin!

Abi   You want some more juice? (**Abi** *goes into the kitchen.*)

Masie   'No more time for foolishness girl, you marrying my boy, that carry responsibilities.' Only thing she ever bin right about. We didn't wish hard enough girl.

Abi   We were young we thought we could rule the world, or you did.

Masie   Don't you think we could of? What happened to our plans Abi, the club?

Abi   How's Ferdy?

Masie   Ferdy?

Abi   Your husband.

Masie   You're still hiding girl, at your age.

Abi   I'm just asking how he is.

Masie   Ferdy's fine.

Abi   He can't be just *fine*! I mean you sure he doesn't mind you staying here for a while? You should be together now.

Masie   Save your sympathy Abigail, Ferdy won't be lonely.

Sound of people calling out the name Shanelle.

Masie   What's wrong?

Abi   Nothing.

Masie   Are you sure?

Abi   I'm fed up. Oh Masie, is this what it feels like?

Masie   What?

Abi   Getting old?

Masie   I don't know. Stand up.

Abi   Excuse me?

Masie   Stand up I say.

Abi   For what?

Masie   I'm tired of letting you make me feel miserable.

Abi   I'm doing that?

Masie   Yes, now stand up! Right, come on let's play.

Abi   We can't, not no more.

Masie   This will make everything better. You see that plank, that's our bat. (*Rolls up* **Danni**'s *paper.*) And this our ball.

Abi   I can't do this.

Masie   Stand over there, be ready to hit that ball, score a six like the old days.

Abi   Masie, I can't do it.

Masie   Eye on the ball, like Charlie Bennett say.

Abi   Are you listening to me?

Masie   No now bat.

Abi   Masie . . .

Masie   I'm bowling.

Masie *bowls,* **Abi** *misses completely.*

Abi   You see?

Masie   You know wat your problem is?

Abi   No but you're gonna tell me.

Masie   You stopped wishing. (*Looking around.*) In a big way. I bat. (*They exchange places.*)

Abi   You know how I feel.

Masie   I can't believe you are still twisting up inside over that. Miss Tyler has been dead for years, why are you still letting her get to you?

Abi   Don't say that woman's name to me!

Masie   Miss Tyler, oh Miss Tyler!

Abi   Stop it.

Masie (*indicating where she wants the ball to be thrown*)   Look just give it to me there, if you can manage that.

Abi   I suppose you never stopped wishing.

Masie   Never. Bowl.

Abi   No! I gotta get dinner ready.

Masie   Gotta go hide you mean.

Abi   If you like!

Abi *leaves.* **Masie** *smiles to herself. She's still got it. She waves the bat a bit more, hitting imaginary ball.*

Masie   Pow, pow, pow! The No Boys Cricket Club! (*Laughs.*)

Masie *stops playing when she sees a badly beaten up* **Danni** *followed by* **Faye**.

Masie   Oh lord what happened here?

Faye   Nuttin, she fell over.

Masie   Girl don't gimme that, I know a beat up girl when I see one.

Faye   What do you know?

Masie   What's your mama gonna say?

Faye   Don't tell her, I don't want her startin' on me.

Abi *comes out.*

Abi   Dannielle, oh my God Dannielle.

Danni   Now don't start Mum I can explain.

Abi   No need. Gangfights Masie, that's what it's about, damn stupid brawling for stupid girls.

Danni   Mum will you leave it.

Abi   No child I will not leave it. (*To* **Faye**.) This is all your fault.

Faye   Of course.

Abi   I don't see no blood on you.

Faye   I wasn't fighting.

Abi   Of course!

Faye   I'm outta here. (*Climbing over the fence.*)

Abi   Yes, don't you have a baby to look after?

Faye   See you tomorrow Danni. (*Enters her house.*)

Abi   Come here. (*Checking her face.*)

Danni   Mum don't fuss.

Abi   Keep still.

Danni (*pushing her away*)   I'm OK! You always showing me up?

Abi   Me?

Danni   You!

Abi   Well you're the one who's been fighting.

Danni   Why do you keep making a show of me, why do you let Michael run rings around you?

Abi   I'm your mother, you answer my questions.

Danni   Shanelle was slagging you off, and it's not just her.

Abi   That's no excuse for brawling on the streets like some dirty animal.

Danni   Oh Mum will you stop, come on you must know what I'm talking about. You can't be that stupid.

Abi   Don't you . . .

Danni   Well are you?

Abi   I don't want you seeing that Faye any more.

Danni   Yeah that's it, turn it around, avoid the question.

Abi   Dannielle . . .

Danni   Ask me what I'm talking about. Why can't you do that?

Abi   Right, thass . . .

Danni (*pre-empting*)   Thass it . . .

Abi   I'm . . .

Danni   . . . I'm done . . .

Abi   I'm not going to say . . .

Danni   . . . say any more!

Danni *goes inside.*

Abi   Damn it!

Masie   I know how you feel girl.

Abi   Don't say that.

Masie   I begged him and I begged him, until I couldn't speak, not to go with his friends, cos deep down I knew he wasn't coming back.

Abi   Oh Lord.

Masie   I know how you feel.

Abi   I'm at my wits' end with the pair of them, you lost your only boy, how can you be so calm?

Masie   Abigail, when was the last time you really thought about home?

Abi   What?

Masie   The truth now.

Abi   Why?

Masie   Come on tell me.

Abi   A few days ago when I got your letter. I was out here, and we, us. . .

Masie   Us?

Abi   It's crazy, it's like I saw the team playing. There was you, me, Jenny, Cita, everybody. I think we were winning.

Masie   You think?

Abi   I scored a six and then. . .

Masie   Wat, come on, wat?

Abi   She turned around.

Masie   Who?

Abi   Me. It was like I was looking right at myself.

Masie   Darling the same thing happened to me, well almost. It's not crazy at all. Abi I swear to you at the funeral reception, I shut my eyes for a minute, when I opened them, I found myself standing right in the middle of Lambert Street.

Abi Lambert Street!

Masie I swear to God. I saw my house. You remember that time I was stayin' with Uncle Ed. I saw myself climbing outta the window, Uncle Ed must have been drunk again. I walked right up the street to your house. You were sitting on the porch crying cos Miss Tyler had upset you again, I wanted to put my arms around you, then he pulled me.

Abi Who?

Masie Ferdy! Always spoiling my fun, he woke me up.

Abi There you see, you musta bin dreaming.

Masie But I tell you it was real. I was there. And the feeling I had, oh God, Abi it was like happiness itself was giving me one huge cuddle. I've never felt that good, I was so angry wid him, day and night since, I wanted to go back.

Abi So why haven't you?

Masie Because I need your help.

Abi Help?

Masie Your one was just as strong as mine, perhaps stronger, we can both go back.

Abi And do what?

Masie I don't know. Let's do all the worrying when we get there.

Abi No, let's go and put you to bed.

Masie I'm not joking here. I think we can do it, I know we can.

Abi Masie stop talking stupidness.

Masie You wanted to know wat can make me feel better, well this can, just do it.

Abi Oh come on Masie . . .

Masie (*pleading*) Abi . . .

Abi   Now stop that. That doesn't work any more.

Masie   If it doesn't work, put me to bed, call the doctor, let him carry me out in a straitjacket, just do it, please, please.

Abi   Alright, alright. So what now?

Masie   Thank you darling. Take my hand in yours, close your eyes, now think and I mean really think. Ya thinkin'?

Abi   I'm thinkin'.

Masie   What do you see?

Abi   You. I'm sitting below your bedroom window, waiting for you to come out. Your Uncle Ed is calling after you, but we run on through Lambert Street. We nearly knock over Miss Stuart, she says summin.

Masie   What?

Abi   I don't know, but I think it's to you.

Masie   Keep thinking Abi.

Abi   What d'you think I'm doing?

Masie   Harder now.

Abi   Alright, I see . . .

Masie   Who, who?

Abi   Miss Tyler, I'm pretending I can't hear her.

Masie (*smiling*)   Good girl, who else?

Abi   There's us, I see Lambert's Field, our cricket field.

At this point **Masie** *opens her eyes. She slowly removes her hands from* **Abi***, who does not notice. Lights rise slowly on the cricket field. Two young girls,* **Jenny** *and* **Cita***, are playing.*

Masie   What else?

Abi   Oh my god, I see Jenny, Cita, Paula. Thelma and Naomi have just showed up on their bikes, the team, I can see the whole team.

Abi *can feel that* **Masie** *is not there. She opens her eyes. She is surprised to find herself standing on the field. She gets up to join* **Abi**.

Masie   Look girl, look where we are, what did I tell you?

Abi   No, no. Everything seems so real. How Masie?

Masie   We wished, it happened, who cares about the in-between? Not me darling. You scared?

Abi   Yes.

Masie   Don't be.

They watch as a young black girl, **Shirley**, *enters, she looks around.*

Masie   Recognise her?

Abi   No, wait a minute, that ain't . . .

Masie/Abi   Insect Shirley! (*They laugh.*)

Masie   She never used the brains God gave her.

Abi   I thought you two were friends.

Masie   Only cos she married my fool of a cousin.

Abi   Still no way to talk about her.

Masie *takes off her shoes and runs over.*

Abi   Masie, don't, Masie . . .

Masie   You alright girl, you look lost.

Abi   Don't.

Shirley   I want to join the club.

Masie   They soon come.

Shirley   I know, thank you.

Abi *pulls her back over.*

Abi   Wat do you think you're doing?

Masie   Just talkin'.

Abi   Well don't.

Masie   You worry too much, just accept it, you'll feel better I promise.

Abi   How would you know?

More of the girls' team enter, including **Young Abi** *and* **Young Masie**. **Masie** *points them out.*

Masie   Now who do you think they are?

Abi   Masie stop this, you hear me, stop it! Wat you tryin' to do, drive me mad?

Masie   Just look at us.

Young Masie   Name?

Shirley   Wat?

Young Masie   Your name!

Shirley   Shirley Hamilton.

Young Abi   Your age?

Shirley   Fifteen.

Young Masie   Address?

Shirley   My wat? . . . You bin to my house plenty of times, come on Masie, you want me in the team or not.

Young Abi   Go practise wid Jenny and Cita, we're gonna have a game in a minute.

The girls giggle. **Masie** *laughs also.*

Masie   What were we like? Abi will you come on, this is not my doing.

Abi   And my arse is blue. Stop this now you hear me?

Masie   You better keep your voice down.

Abi   I will not.

Masie   They are looking at us.

Abi   No.

Masie   They're coming over.

Abi   No!

Young Masie   Morning Miss May.

Masie   Morning girls.

Abi   Miss May?

Masie   How you doing sweetiepie?

Young Masie   Oh I'm fine.

Masie   You got quite a team here.

Young Masie   We need them. Got a game coming up real soon.

Masie   Clanton Street.

Young Masie   You know about that?

Masie   Word gets around.

Young Masie   We're gonna beat them good.

Masie   I know you will. (*She feels* **Abi**'s *glare.*) You will!

Young Masie (*to* **Abi**)   Masie Williams.

Abi (*nervous*)   Pleased to meet you.

Young Abi   Abigail Sandford.

Abi   Abi . . . Miss Carter.

Masie   Well shake hands nuh?

Abi *is terrified, they shake hands but* **Young Abi** *is reluctant to let go.*

Young Abi   I know you, don't I?

Abi   No we haven't met.

Young Abi   Yeah we have.

Abi   I said no!

Young Abi   Alright.

Masie   Masie, you bin practising that move wid the ball I taught you?

Young Masie   Oh yes, come let me show you.

Abi   Wait I wan' to talk to you Miss May!

Masie   Later yeah.

Abi   Now!

Masie   Later.

They go off, leaving the two **Abi**s *alone.*

Young Masie (*offstage*)   Team, come. You too Insect Shirley.

The girls laugh as they exit as well.

Young Abi   Don't worry, Masie does that to me all the time. She never listens to a word I say.

Abi   This is crazy.

Young Abi   Wat you say?

Abi   Nothing.

Young Abi   Please don't bite off my head again, but I do know you. Did you know my mother, Gloria Sandford?

Abi   No! Yes, I knew your mother.

Young Abi   She died last year you know.

Abi   I'm sorry.

Young Abi   It's alright. So you want to practise with me?

Abi   Oh no dear, I'm not that good.

Young Abi   Come on, I bet you're wicked like Miss May.

Abi   She bin teachin' you then?

Young Abi   Oh yes, mostly Masie though, them two are like that, everytime she comes.

Abi   When did you first meet her?

Young Abi   A few months back. I didn't like her at first, she fills Masie's head with a lot of nonsense.

Abi   Like what?

Young Abi   The club. Sayin' we're gonna play forever, be famous around the world. Masie laps it all up.

Abi   She's a dreamer.

Young Abi   You know.

They catch each other's eyes.

Abi   You remind me of someone I used to know.

Young Abi   Did she play?

Abi   Oh yes.

Young Abi   Any good?

Abi   The best.

Young Abi   Well, no more cricket for me. My daddy's coming back this weekend. Gotta persuade him to stay here, instead of working up in the country, going to show him I'm a good girl. Miss Tyler will have to leave me alone, you know Miss Tyler?

Abi   Oh yes I know her.

Young Abi   Tell me something. Did she have black teeth even when she was little?

Abi   Abigail!

Young Abi   Sorry shouldn't have said that.

Abi   Yes, she did actually. (*They laugh.*)

Young Abi   I'm gonna be a nurse.

Abi   Thass nice, but your daddy will have summin to say about that.

Young Abi   No he won't. He's gonna be proud.

Abi   Why are you telling me all this?

Young Abi   Daddy always taught me to be a friend to everyone I meet, didn't you know I'm a country girl!

Abi (*laughs*)   Of course! Forget about your daddy for a minute, why are you telling me this?

Young Abi   Because . . .

Abi   I think you should play.

Young Abi   Why?

Abi   You just should.

Young Abi   But my plans?

Abi   Plans don't work out.

Young Abi   Sure they will. Listen right, my dream's this . . .

Abi   Don't say another word to me about it. This has gone on far enough.

Young Abi   What has?

Abi   Forget you ever saw me Abi alright, enjoy your family, enjoy your gift from your father . . .

Young Abi   Who are you?

Abi   Miss May, Miss May!

Young Abi   Wait, who are you? Tell me.

Abi   I'm so sorry.

Young Abi   For what?

Abi   Everything . . . nothing!

The two **Masie***s arrive.*

Abi   We are leaving.

Masie   Abi . . .

Abi   Right now!

Young Abi   No, answer my question.

Young Masie   Come Abi, leave them alone.

Young Abi   Let me go Masie. (*To* **Abi**.) I want to know who you are.

Abi   We're leaving.

Young Masie   Come on Abi.

Young Abi   Lemme go.

Young Masie   You wan' me to punch you out?

Young Abi   Try it!

Abi *refuses to look at her younger self.*

Young Abi (*to* **Young Masie**)   Move from me!

She runs off.

Abi   I want to go.

Masie   What happened?

Abi   She was going on and on about her father.

Masie   And that wasn't telling you something?

Abi   No!

Masie   I don't believe you.

Abi   I don't care.

Masie   Abigail, don't you see this is for you as well as for me. It's not your fault your mother died.

Abi   Shut up about that.

Masie   No! She caught you sneaking off school with me, she was giving you the beating of your life, you prayed for her to stop.

Abi   Then she died, right in front of me.

Masie   You know she had a bad heart.

Abi   No Masie no! You're a damn liar. You've bin here before, Lord knows how many times.

Masie   Alright yes.

Abi   How? What is going on?

Masie   What does it matter? There's a lot of pain inside you girl.

Abi   There is nothing inside of me.

Masie   So you've forgiven your father for abandoning you?

Abi   Why are you doing this to me?

Masie   Forget about all of them. Look over there, Jenny Vincent, she's bin married for thirty odd years, working as a cleaner in some office can never afford to buy her own home. Connie Phillips, still hanging around Lambert Street looking for a man, any man at her age.

Abi   I know about Jenny and Connie.

Masie   Then you must know if you had stayed in the team we would never have lost that game against the Clanton boys.

Abi   Oh Masie. You really believe me scoring some sixes would have changed our lives? Come off it.

Masie   Susie Tanner, Maggie Gordon, Shirley Hamilton, after that game they all scatter to the winds. Look what happened to them, look what happened to you.

Abi   No. I don't know how you did it and I don't care.

Masie   Look me in the eye and tell me you don't want this.

Abi   I don't want it.

Masie   You disappoint me.

Abi   I'm going back. You hear me? I said . . .

Masie   Alright fine!

Act Two

Scene One

London, early morning, three days later. **Abi** *is watering her plants. She is quietly singing to herself.* **Danni** *enters from the house carrying her hold-all.*

Danni   What you doing up so early?

Abi   The only time I can see you these days. No breakfast again? You should always make time to eat in the mornings sweetheart.

Danni   I'm gonna miss my bus.

Abi   Oh to hell with the bus, miss college for the day.

Danni   And muck up my exams? Can't have that Mum.

Abi   Look child I know it's not the first time you've missed college. So you can make time for me. What's all this business with Shanelle?

Danni   What business?

Abi   Come on.

Danni   Come on what?

Abi   Why are you doing this?

Danni   Oh Mum don't talk like that.

Abi   Like what?

Danni   Like you're begging. It's no wonder they laugh at you.

Abi   Well pardon me.

Danni   I do thass the problem. If you knew I was bunking off college, how come you didn't say nuttin?

Abi   What, me sticking my nose into your affairs, showing you up? Can't have that Danni.

Danni   It would have been something.

Abi   You never want me to help you, never. Remember that time when you were four, and you wanted to sew a button on your dress all by yourself? 'I can do it Mum, I can do it.' Dannielle I am not a mindreader. How am I supposed to know?

Danni   Why did you let Michael back in?

Abi   Not the damn room again.

Danni   I'm fed up, every time him and Judith split up, it's always the same.

Abi   We have an agreement, he promised there'll be no trouble this time.

Danni   Yeah right.

Abi   What am I supposed to do, fling him out on the street?

Danni   We're not talking car radios and mobile phones Mum. You know what's getting into now, don't you? But you just stand there doing nuttin.

Abi   Oh stop your noise.

Danni   I wouldn't get as many bruises.

Abi   Don't use Michael as an excuse for your fighting, it's she. (*Pointing over to next door.*) That mouth on legs.

Danni   That's right blame Faye.

Abi   Well you want to blame Michael.

Danni   Stop hiding will you?

Abi   I'm not hiding. I am fed up with everyone trying to climb inside my head.

Danni   What the hell are you talking about?

Abi You're rude you know.

Danni And you only care about yourself.

Abi And you only care about having your dinner on the table.

Danni Mum you can't even cook properly.

Abi (*outraged*) What! (*Throwing her hold-all.*) Go and get your bus Danni now!

Danni Right!

Danni *leaves.*

Abi (*back to watering the plants*) Can't cook, can't cook? Yes you look like you're starving.

Masie *enters, she sees* **Abi** *and goes to walk back in.*

Abi Where you going Masie?

Masie For a walk.

Abi Another one? Wat is it about here you find so fascinating? Twenty-odd years I've been living here, and I still hate the damn place.

Masie So move.

Abi And go where? Are you still vex with me?

Masie You didn't even try to like it.

Abi Masie Williams you never know when to stop. There she was, fifteen years old, planning out her whole life, talking about her father. I don't need to hear that.

Masie What were you and Danni fighting about?

Abi The generation gap, and all that's in it.

Masie You should have made her play.

Abi Danni?

Masie No, you, her, Abi!

Abi   You're wrong.

Masie   Trust me, watch all your problems go away.

Abi   Oh Masie I can't. Where are you going?

Masie   Nowhere! (*She stops.*) Want some tea?

Abi   Yeah I would love some.

Masie *goes back in.* **Abi** *clocks* **Faye** *coming out.*

Faye   Yes?

Abi   Wat you bin doin' to my daughter?

Faye   I ain't done nuttin to her.

Abi   You keep on dragging her into trouble, leave her alone you hear me? Worry about yourself for a change.

Faye   Myself?

Abi   You call yourself a mother? You're a disgrace.

Faye   Don't talk like you know me, you're not my mum, you not my mum, you got no right.

Abi   I work for a living, I've got plenty right to . . .

Faye   No not while your precious little boy is feeding half the crackheads around here with shit you don't.

Abi   What you saying?

Faye   Oh yeah, right. Like you know nothing. You say I'm a disgrace.

Abi   You little bitch.

Faye   Fuck off. (*Goes in.*)

Abi   I control my house, my kids. You hear me!

She stops and holds her head in her hands. **Ferdy**, **Masie**'s *husband, leans over the gate.*

Ferdy   Psst. Excuse me madam, but you wouldn't mind telling me where I might find a couple of exciting women for some morning fun eh?

Abi   Well here is one, come, let me take a good look at you.

Ferdy *enters the garden, they laugh.*

Ferdy   How's my girl?

Abi   Ferdy Watson get yourself over here. (*They embrace.*) It's about time.

Ferdy   Hey, traffic was a bitch you know.

Abi   How you feeling?

Ferdy   Oh fine, fine.

Abi   Vanessa, Claudia?

Ferdy   Coping, better than we. Hey hey hold on, girl you bin crying. Is who upset my Abigail? Tell me now.

Abi   Enough of your hard man act. Worry about your wife.

Ferdy   Where is she?

Abi   She soon come. You bring the pictures I asked you?

Ferdy (*hands them over*)   Here.

Abi   Oh, she is beautiful.

Ferdy   Course, takes after her grandpa.

Abi   Oh hush.

Ferdy   Look at the next one.

Abi   Oh Lord.

Ferdy (*giggling*)   Thass my favourite one.

Abi   Who put that hat on the poor little thing?

Ferdy   Vanessa, the little scamp.

Abi   I wonder who she get that from?

Ferdy (*innocent*)   Me?

Abi   You!

Masie *enters carrying two mugs.*

Ferdy   How's my favourite girl?

Masie   What are you doing here?

Ferdy   I've come to see you of course. Didn't Abi say I was coming?

Masie (*to* **Abi**)   And you moan to me about interfering with your life.

Ferdy   What she say?

Abi   Nothing.

Ferdy   Let me help you wid that.

Masie   I can do it.

Ferdy   OK. Oh. Tea. That's nice.

Masie   Good one Ferdy.

Abi   I'll go inside and make you some.

Masie   You do that Abigail.

Ferdy   You know I wouldn't mind summin a little stronger.

Abi   Alright, one black coffee.

Ferdy (*pretending to be glad*)   Nice.

Abi *goes.*

Masie   Summin a little stronger, you're driving aren't you?

Ferdy   Yeah but . . .

Masie   But? You expect me to drive you home rat-arsed again.

Ferdy   No.

Masie   Yes.

Ferdy   What kind of greeting is this? I've just come to see you, you're my wife remember. So how are you, you alright?

Masie   Yes!

Ferdy   Everyone bin askin' at the church for you, especially the Reverend.

Masie   Thass nice.

Ferdy   Vanessa passed her exams.

Masie   Don't do this.

Ferdy   Do what?

Masie   Don't go around the block like you always do, what do you want?

Ferdy   Of all the stupid . . . you know wat I want, you to come home. You're not the only one who loved him.

Masie   You think that's what it's all about, you're a blind man Ferdy.

Ferdy   Well tell me then.

Masie   I don't have the time.

Ferdy   Masie . . .

Masie   Just go back to your fancy woman and leave me alone.

Ferdy   How many more times do I have to tell you? Lena is not my fancy woman. We were just talkin' and ting . . .

Masie   Did you show her?

Ferdy   Show her what?

Masie   Your ting?

Ferdy   Don't get nasty alright. Nothing happened.

Masie   What kinda fool do you think I am? Thirty-odd
years of marriage Ferdy and you think I don't recognise the
'I hope Masie doesn't find out' face? You're wearing it now
sweetheart. It was embarrassing enough when you were our
son's age, now it's just boring and pathetic.

Ferdy   He has a name you know, our son.

Masie   I know.

Ferdy   Then use it! We had a son named Jeffrey. You still
blame me don't you?

Masie   You could've stopped him, he would have listened
to you.

Ferdy   Them white boys were nothing but trash.

Masie   You should have stopped him.

Ferdy   Why, I'm proud of what he did!

Masie   Proud? Proud he's dead? He should have gone to
the police.

Ferdy   What century you living in woman? It's our war,
we fight it ourselves.

Masie   Shut up, shut up, save that rubbish for the ones
who believe it. (*Mocking him.*) Fight the war ourselves, you
bin sniffing Vanessa's Tipp-Ex?

Ferdy   You're wrong.

Masie   Course I am. I'm always wrong. Like I was wrong
putting him in that school, five miles from where we lived, I
was wrong not letting his friends come into our home, I was
wrong when I yelled at him for losing the best job he ever
had, like I was wrong on the night he . . . Yes Ferdy I'm
always wrong.

Ferdy   We can't go on like this. I can't keep lying to
Vanessa. She ain't stupid you know, Claudia is worried too.

Masie   That makes a change. I suppose as usual you that went to see her. Knew it. She's too good for us now ain't it?

Ferdy   Will you please come home?

Masie   You know when I held him in my arms for the first time, it was the only real time I believed I could bury what I left behind, I remember whispering to his ear, I will protect you forever my sweet, but later I could see in his eyes, him plotting to get what he could out of me.

Ferdy   Stop this talk.

Masie   You whisked him away, outta my arms, moulded him into your image, you moulded all of them. I told him I'd protect him, you made a liar out of me. Well to hell with you, Claudia, the baby, Vanessa, Jeffrey!

Ferdy   I don't believe you said that.

Masie   Then I'll say it again. To hell with Jeffrey!

Ferdy   Don't! We need you.

Masie   I need you to get out of my sight.

Ferdy   You want a doctor.

Masie   And why is that?

Ferdy   Abi was sayin' how you bin daydreaming again.

Masie   That girl tell more lies than me. Ferdy will you please go?

Ferdy   You coming home or not? Last chance.

Masie   Wat have I told you about your macho act, it don't work on me. But don't worry my love, I'm coming home, but not to Streatham.

Ferdy   What you sayin' now?

Masie   Nothing.

Ferdy   Masie . . .

Masie   Leave me alone!

Scene Two

The same location, one hour later. **Abi** *is outside knitting. Sound of furniture being smashed around.* **Abi** *jumps. She stops what she is doing and waits nervously.* **Michael** *steams outside.*

Michael   Mum have you bin in my room? Have you bin in my room? What have I told you about that?

Abi   This is still my house.

Michael   Mum where are they? Where are they?

Abi   You're dealing drugs!

Michael   Don't tell me my business.

Abi   My God what have I done?

Michael   Just gimme them.

Abi   Why Michael?

Michael   Mum gimme them.

Abi   Why are you punishing me?

Michael   What? You're bloody mad.

Abi   You want to hear me beg you?

Michael   Look I ain't got time for this, not today.

Abi   Is this why Judith won't let you see Patrick?

Michael   Forget about Patrick, Mum.

Abi   I'm asking you a question.

Michael   Shut up and listen for once, forget about Patrick. He ain't coming round no more.

Abi   Why is that?

Michael   The stuff Mum.

Abi   Answer my question.

Michael   She's got herself a new man.

Abi   So?

Michael   So he wears a suit to work, and Patrick adores him.

Abi   You're still his father.

Michael   Not no more. He's got himself a new daddy.

Abi   That's not right at all.

Michael   So what would you prefer then, him coming round and you knowing what you know? That don't make you a very good grandma.

Abi   You think you can push every girl around like you do me. I warned you. How the hell can Patrick look up to you when . . . ?

Michael   It's always him isn't it!

Abi   You are a disgrace!

Michael   What is this huh? We're Sandfords Mum, we don't care about anything. You taught me well.

Abi   He will always be your son.

Michael   The boy's well out of it.

Abi   That isn't true. Listen to me . . .

Michael   No, tell me where did you hide them? Don't make me tear this place apart Mum please.

Abi   I flushed them.

Michael   No, no you didn't.

Abi   Oh yes.

Michael   No, no! No. You got any idea how much they're worth, any idea, Jesus! (*Swings his arm around, accidently hitting* **Abi**.) Mum, Mum, I'm sorry.

Abi   It's alright, leave me.

Michael   If I hit you for real, you wouldn't stand up.

Abi   I have knitting to do.

Michael   It was an accident.

Abi   Making Danni a sweater, make up for her birthday.

Michael   You know where it's going to end up, in the bin. You know Danni likes to get her own clothes, but you still do it, nothing sinks in. Wat am I talkin' to you for? You don't know how to. You're nuttin without Dad. All you do is go on about sweet Jamaica. Even when Dad was here you did the same, he gave up plenty too you know. All you did was make a fool of him. You wanna talk about fools. All I see is some sad old woman, and she ain't much. (**Michael** *exits.*)

Abi *tries to carry on knitting; she gives up and throws it to the floor.* **Masie** *comes out.*

Abi   Masie?

Masie   I'm not talking to you.

Abi   I had to do something.

Masie   You didn't have to go behind my back.

Abi   Talk to me please.

Masie   About wat?

Abi   Anything.

Masie   I haven' got time alright, I'll do it on my own . . . (*Notices* **Abi**'s *lip*.) Wat happened to you, let me see Abi, Michael do this, are things this bad?

Abi   He didn't mean it, at least I think . . . Oh Masie I wish I could just trade it all in you know; job, home, children, the lot. I've got nothing left to give them. You know when Teddy died, I thought 'I'm free'. When I was alone in my bedroom I threw all of his things off the dressing table and our wedding picture right across the room. Already my head was filling up with ideas of going back home, study to be a nurse, Miss Tyler was dead,

Daddy was gone, I was free, but soon as I turned around I saw little Michael by the door, and girl the look in his eyes, I'm a walking, talking curse.

Masie   No you're not.

Abi   But he came looking for me, I should have put my arm around him, wiped his tears, I'm his mother. I haven't done much of a job, for either of them.

Masie   Listen girl you are no curse. You are Abigail Sandford, devil with a bat. You couldn't be a curse to anyone.

Abi   You always see the best in me Masie Williams.

Masie   Someone has to.

Abi   I don't want to lose you.

Masie   Who says you do?

Abi   Oh Masie, is this what it feels like?

Masie   What?

Abi   Losing our minds?

Masie   Do you think we have?

Abi   It seemed real to me.

Masie   So what are you saying?

Abi   You want some company?

Masie   Well this is a turnaround. Take my hand in yours, close your eyes, now think.

Abi   I'm thinking.

Scene Three

The cricket field, Kingston. The match is in full swing. **Young Masie** *is watching; she is the only one taking an interest in the game.* **Jenny** *and* **Shirley** *are sitting alongside her.*

Young Masie (*calling out*)   Watch the ball now Cita, hit it y' hearing me? Me say hit it! Now run girl!

Jenny   John Wayne! Girl shut your mout, Audie Murphy is the best cowboy that ever lived.

Shirley   Could he fight like John Wayne, draw up his six shooter like John Wayne can? No.

Jenny   Shirley I'm only gonna say one thing to you right, in one film I see Audie Murphy shoot down train robbers, become sheriff, and wipe out a tribe of dem nasty Apache!

Shirley   Wat movie?

Jenny   I don't remember.

Shirley   G'way!

Young Masie   You two here to play or not? Jenny you're up next, be ready.

Shirley   Wass the point, they're beating us good you know.

Young Masie   We can still win this, I don't want to hear dem say . . . girls can't play, you hear me.

Clanton Street Boys (*offstage*)   Howzat!

Shirley   Masie we need a miracle.

Jenny   We need Abi.

Masie   Just shut up!

Lights on **Abi**. **Young Masie** *and the girls freeze.* **Abi** *is holding her shoes, she looks very happy as she sings to herself.*

Abi   Masie and I spent ages visiting our old haunts, that sorta thing. All the way down Lambert Street we went; we saw Miss Stuart still sitting on her stool on the corner, (*laughs*) the Brewster boys, Masie's house, my house. It hadn't changed a bit, every door, every window looked exactly the same. I never liked that place you know, it was her house, Miss Tyler's! Staring at it made me remember the day we first moved there. I was seven and we left the country to live in Kingston, and I remember seeing this little summin of a house perched on this hill. I say to myself 'I have to walk up that (*Tuts.*) wid me only in sandals'. So I cried blue murder to my daddy saying 'I don't want to go up there!' Moma yelled 'Stop your foolishness!' But I cried and I cried you see. Moma was rolling up her sleeves, ready to give me a slap when Daddy turned round and say 'I'll tell you what, you take my shoes and I take yours'. (*Laughs.*) So I put his shoes on, and straight up the hill I went, Mummy of course thought we were playing the arse of ourselves, but we just laughed, couldn't stop. Oh, sweet Jamaica. (*Puts her arms around herself, giving herself a cuddle.*) Masie was right. I feel, reunited wid my soul. (*Laughs.*) 'Hello soul, hello Abi. Long time no hear girl!' Long time.

Masie *comes up behind* **Abi**.

Masie   Talkin' to yourself, people will think you're mad girl.

Abi   Oh hush. You know Masie you're right. Why in God's name did we ever want to leave?

Masie   We got work to do. Come on!

Abi   Come on!

Clanton Street Boys (*offstage*)   Out!

Abi *and* **Masie** *go over to where the game is playing.* **Jenny** *goes out to bat.* **Cita** *joins the girls.*

Young Masie   Watch the ball, you hear me Jenny? Just hit the ball.

Jenny   I hear you.

Cita   See that boy bowling, 'im nice.

Young Masie   You here to play or not?

Cita   Ease up nah!

Young Masie   Hey! Just don't say a word to me.

Shirley   Can I go to the toilet please?

Young Masie   Just get outta my sight. Damn you Abi!

Masie *stares at her friend.* **Abi** *feels uncomfortable.*

Masie (*to* **Young Masie**)   Hey girl!

Young Masie   Oh hi Miss May. (*Sound of a ball being hit.*)
Go Jenny!

Masie   How you doing?

Young Masie   Can't you tell?

Masie   You miss Abi don't you?

Young Masie (*to* **Abi**)   Wat did you say to her?

Abi   Me?

Young Masie   She was fine before she spoke to you, fine.

Abi   I think you know it isn't true.

Young Masie   You know wat's gonna happen here, we'll
lose, then I'll lose them.

Masie   Listen to me girl, listen. It's not going to happen,
you gotta wish hard. You hear me? Now come on, you can
still win this. Right Miss C?

Clanton Street Boys (*offstage*)   Howzat!

Young Masie   Shirley you're up, Shirley! I suppose it's
down to me.

Masie   Just keep them busy. Whack the ball straight over
Kingston.

Young Masie   I'll do my best. (*She goes.*)

Abi   Why are you looking at me like that Masie?

Masie   You know wat you have to do.

Abi   Why?

Masie   Why! Widowed, alone, raising two ungrateful pikne? One beats you, your own child.

Abi   Shut up.

Masie   You wouldn't be here if you didn't want this.

Abi   Masie listen.

Masie   No don't tell me you don't want this chance, just don't tell me that. Where you going?

Abi   Far away from you.

Masie   Good, that's good.

Abi   Just leave me alone.

Masie   You find her Abi, make her play.

Scene Four

Kingston. **Young Abi** *is sitting alone on the beach writing a letter.*

Young Abi   . . . and thank you for sending me the poetry book Daddy, it was lovely. I'm sorry as well that you couldn't come down that time, I know you're busy. I really miss you though. I hope you're looking after yourself or I'll have to come up there. So from now on, no more foolishness from me. I'll get on wid school, get married – you best keep yourself fit cos you're gonna get plenty grandchildren. No more of me thinking of myself, gonna make you happy Daddy. (**Abi** *enters at this point.*) Why aren't you here . . .

Young Abi/Abi   I want you here.

Young Abi *turns around quickly.*

Abi   It's only me.

Young Abi   How did you find me.

Abi   I knew you'd be here.

Young Abi   But how? No one knows, this is where I . . .

Abi   Write letters to your Daddy.

Young Abi   You know too much about me.

Abi   Doesn't that tell you something?

Young Abi   If it did would I be askin'?

Abi *laughs.*

Young Abi   Wat, stop that, wat?

Abi   Still got an answer for everything. How I've missed that.

Young Abi   You're no friend of my mother's.

Abi   Correct.

Young Abi   So who are you?

Abi   The team are getting well beat you know.

Young Abi   That's not my problem any more.

Abi   Sweetheart I know wat you're going through, but turning your back on your friends won't help you believe me.

Young Abi   Believe you?

Abi   Abi listen, we don't have much time.

Young Abi   I'm not going to listen to you.

Abi   Look at your letter, look at it. (*Reciting.*) 'Dear Daddy, I've got some good news for you. I've finally left that stupid ol' cricket team.'

Young Abi *screws up the letter and steps away, terrified.*

Young Abi   You get away from me.

Abi (*still reciting*)   I've decided that you and Miss Tyler were right all along.

Young Abi   You're a damn crazy woman.

Abi   You just wait till you see me next. And thank you for sending me the poetry book Daddy, it was lovely.

Young Abi (*screams*)   Move from me!

Abi   . . . I'm sorry as well that you couldn't come down that time . . .

Abi *grabs the young girl's arm and rolls up her sleeve.*

Young Abi   Lemme go, you wan' me to punch you out?

Abi   Punch me? You got that scar on your arm when you were nine years old. Old man Rivers's dog bite you, right? (*Rolls up her sleeve.*) See?

Young Abi   No.

Abi   Look at me, look into my eyes, look!

Young Abi (*frantic.*)   No I say!

Young Abi *tries to run,* **Abi** *grabs her.*

Abi   Are you scared? Answer me, are you scared?

Young Abi   Yes.

Abi   Don't be.

Young Abi   I know, somehow I . . . (*Touches* **Abi**'s *scar on her arm but pulls away.*) How? I don't understand, how can you be here? Why are you here?

Abi   To escape, I wanted to see home again, to see you. I'm giving you a chance to change things.

Young Abi   What things?

Abi   Your life Abi.

Young Abi   How?

Abi   You musn't give up on yourself.

Young Abi   But I'm not going to, you must know that.

Abi   And you have to play the game.

Young Abi   Why? I know what I'm doing.

Abi   You don't. You only want what other people want you to have. Miss Tyler, your daddy . . .

Young Abi   No this ain't right at all, I'm gonna go University, I'm gonna . . .

Abi   That won't happen. Everything started from here Abi. Miss Tyler won't stop you know, she's gonna keep on making your life hell, an' you're so wrapped up in worrying after Daddy and working in her shop day and night. You'll be doing the right thing for everybody, Abigail, except yourself. Maybe if you had just carried on playing . . .

Young Abi   You're talking shit!

Abi   Abigail!

Young Abi   Wat, you never said shit before?

Abi   How much more proof do you want?

Young Abi   Plenty, about givin' up on myself.

Abi   You want to hear how I cried myself to sleep night after night cos Miss Tyler tell me Daddy don't love me? And shall I tell you how you really feel? You believe Daddy blames you for Moma's death.

Young Abi   Alright alright. Now tell me about my dream.

Abi (*laughs*)   Your dream.

Young Abi   My dream! The one that keeps me going, come on, alright, I can see myself when I'm older so happy, enjoying life and everything else around me. No Miss Tyler, nobody, there are times when I can't wait to get there, to be you, you bitch!

Abi   What did you just say?

Young Abi   You did it, didn't you, you gave up, that's why you're here.

Abi   Don't speak that way to me.

Young Abi   Yes, oh yes.

Abi   I mean it.

Young Abi   Tell me then.

Abi   Things are different where I come from, pressure you wouldn't believe.

Young Abi   You should have held on. So wat are you then? Not a nurse I take it. Come on, someone's cleaner, summin like that.

Abi   No.

Young Abi   You married? Children? To who, who?

Abi   Teddy Carter.

Young Abi   Oh Jesus! You mean to say I have pikne who look like him? What happened to my dream? How could you let this happen?

Abi   We both did. I'm telling you. Soon Abi you won't even care. Four years from now you're gonna marry Teddy, believe it or not, right, he does grow to be a kind and decent man but you won't love him. Play the game. Hit some sixes, for you, Masie, the whole team. Abi please.

Young Abi   Now I know who's really talkin'.

Abi (*impatient*)   Me!

Young Abi   Masie Williams. Not even that has changed, she still got you doing wat she wants. I thought you would have the strength to stand up to her by now.

Abi   But she's right about this.

Young Abi   You really think so?

Abi   Yes!

Young Abi   We are talkin' about the same Masie? The one who hid from Pearl Daniels in my backyard and begged me to beat up the girl? Or the one who always copies my homework? Listen I love Masie like a sister, but you really think she is doing this for us?

Abi   But I've never bin the same since I came to England. Day by day everything just went out of me. I can't even hit a ball now.

Young Abi   I can't believe you've forgotten so much. Who taught us how to play in the first place?

Abi   Big Charlie Bennett.

Young Abi   . . . Big Charlie Bennett. 'Now remember girl, hold the ball firmly in your palm, like so. An' when you bat, never take your eyes offa it, never.' When we moved from the country did we forget everything he taught us?

Abi   Of course not.

Young Abi   So why you forget now? You are Abigail Rosemary Sandford.

Abi   I know who I am.

Young Abi   Do you?

Young Abi *searches around the beach.*

Young Abi   There's always something. Ah!

Young Abi *finds some paper, rolls it up into a ball, and a piece of wood.*

Abi   What are you doing?

Young Abi   I'm going to bowl, you (*hands her the wood*) are going to bat.

Abi   No I can't do this any more. You're young.

Young Abi   You're pathetic.

Abi   You have been with me every day and night, what do you want me to say, I'm sorry?

Young Abi   Don't be sorry, hit the ball.

Young Abi *bowls,* **Abi** *misses it completely.* **Young Abi** *says nothing when getting the ball of paper back.*

Young Abi   Again.

Abi   We are wasting time.

Young Abi   Again.

Abi   It should be you. Come on Abi.

Young Abi   You see me? This Abigail Sandford would never give up. I know who I am, I don't know you. I hate you.

Abi   Then you must hate yourself.

Young Abi   You best hit this damn ball.

Abi (*fierce*)   Alright!

Abi *catches the ball with the bat and whacks the ball clean over. She feels something.*

Abi   Did I just do that?

Young Abi   Yes! You see, you see.

Abi   But Jesus Christ.

Young Abi   You never lose a gift like that.

Abi   But Jesus Christ!

Young Abi   How does the dream look now? (**Abi** *is beaming.*) I love that smile.

Abi   Throw me another one, I gotta tell myself that was no fluke.

Young Abi   That was no fluke. (*Taking the piece of wood from her.*) And I think you know. (*Laughs.*)

Abi   What?

Young Abi   Teddy Carter?

Abi   Worry about your children, I tell you Dannielle and Michael . . .

Young Abi   No, don't say any more.

Abi   Wat about the team, Masie?

Young Abi   They'll just have to learn, like we? Masie won't like that.

Abi   Nor will Miss May.

Young Abi   Yours? You mean to say, Miss May is . . .

Abi   Yes.

Young Abi   Should have known.

Abi   You think your Masie knows?

Young Abi   She's keeping it a secret if she does. Wouldn't surprise me.

Abi   Will you just listen to one thing I tell you?

Young Abi   One thing.

Abi   It wasn't your fault Moma died. No matter what that witch Miss Tyler says. You must believe that.

Young Abi   Do you?

Abi   Yes, I think I do now.

Young Abi   Then we don't have a problem.

Abi   Where did you learn to be so smart?

Young Abi   Didn't you know . . .

Abi/Young Abi   I'm a country girl! (*They laugh, then embrace.*)

Abi   Oh sweetheart. Come with me.

Young Abi   No, I'll stay here.

Abi   Abigail Sandford does not hide you know.

Young Abi   I'm not hiding from anything.

Abi   So come with me.

Abi *takes the hand of* **Young Abi**. *They stroll off.*

Scene Five

The cricket field, Kingston. **Young Masie** *stands alone. Sound of* **Clanton Street Boys** *laughing and singing.*

Young Masie   Shut up!

Boy   Wha' wrong wid you, can't take losin'?

Young Masie   I can take a lot of things like a stick into the back of your blasted neck!

The **Clanton Street Boys** *laugh and cheer louder, their voices fade away.* **Young Abi** *and* **Abi** *enter.*

Young Masie   So you finally show up then?

Young Abi   Masie . . .

Young Masie   No.

Young Abi   Let me talk to you.

Young Masie   I said leave me!

Young Masie *runs off,* **Young Abi** *goes after her.* **Masie** *enters from the other side.*

Abi   It's over.

Masie   You think I don't know that? You think I was going to stay and watch it happen all over again?

Abi   Let me talk to you.

Masie   We had this conversation before you know, I can see them from here look; you're putting your arm around me telling me why you did it, how your family is so important to you, how we still got time. You were so good I started to believe it. Abi, don't you realise for people like us, there are fewer days ahead than there are behind? You couldn't persuade her, maybe I can.

Abi   Leave her alone.

Masie   Afraid I'll change her mind?

Abi   You're wasting your time, cos if you're talkin' to her, you're talkin' to me.

Masie   Still thinkin' the world will wait for you Mrs Abigail Carter! You can't even see that same world is pushing you into the ground.

Abi   But not you?

Masie   No not me!

Abi   Enough of this. You have a family and they need you.

Masie   What I have is an empty house, and you want me to give up all this again? Who am I Abi – that young feisty go-getter of a girl? I loved those things about me, I miss those things.

Abi   You don't have to, they're right there!

Masie   Or am I some sad old woman who lives to bore her kids, the one they just humour and patronise when they think I'm just rambling on about foolishness? They think we don't know, but we do, don't we?

Abi   Yes.

Masie   You can do wat you want.

Abi   Masie . . .

Masie   Don't worry I won't trouble her, but that is me over there, she needs me.

Abi You'll fail.

Masie Then very little would have been lost.

Abi Don't say that.

Masie Go home Abi.

Abi I'm not going to leave you here.

Masie Fine, stay. (**Abi** *reaches out to touch her,* **Masie** *pushes her away.*) No, I let you put your arm around me before. Just go. And Abi, you know if you can ever afford to come home and go to the cricket field, you might see a very, very old woman waving a bat. You never know girl.

Abi Gimme your hand Masie.

Masie No.

Abi You are coming home with me.

Masie No.

Abi *grabs her, they struggle, hard.*

Masie Abi let me go. Come on now. You wan' me to punch you out?

Abi Try it.

Masie *breaks free.*

Masie Keep an eye on the kids for me. Bye my darling. (*She runs.*)

Abi (*screaming*) Masie!

Scene Six

London, the next morning. Sound of a baby crying, **Faye** *comes out, she lights up a cigarette.*

Faye Oh shut up, please, just shut up.

Faye *is distracted by loud sounds coming from next door. She looks over and sees* **Abi** *dragging a packed suitcase out. They clock each other.*

Faye (*laughs*)   Fuck . . .

Abi   Yes!

Danni (*coming out*)   Mum, what you doing?

Abi   Out of my way child.

Danni   Tell me what you're doing first.

Abi   Will you move?

Abi *goes inside.*

Faye   What's going on?

Danni   You asking me?

Abi *comes out dragging another bag.*

Danni   You're gonna do your back in dragging it like that.

Abi   Danni, Danni, leave me alone.

Danni   Mum will you slow down for a minute will ya? What are you doing with Michael's stuff? Is he moving out or something? Mum don't ignore me. Is Michael moving out?

Abi   Yes.

Danni   He told you?

Abi   No.

Danni   You chucking him out?

Abi   Yes child.

Danni   What for?

Abi   You're not stupid Dannielle.

Faye (*laughs*)   Sorry.

Abi   Go get the other box for me, go on.

Danni *goes.* **Abi** *goes over to* **Faye**.

Faye   Alright, come on, your insult for the day is . . .

Abi   You get my daughter into any more trouble, and I will cut in half every bone in your body.

Faye (*pretending to be aroused*)   Ooooh!

Abi   Yes. Go on, enjoy it. Because I'm telling you now it's gonna be for the last time.

Faye   What?

Abi   Tell that to everybody. (*Turns her back.*)

Faye   What? (*Baby cries.*) Alright, I'm coming.

Faye *goes back in.* **Danni** *comes out.*

Abi   Well put it down.

Danni   Don't you think it's a bit late for this, the assertive mother act?

Abi   No.

Michael *enters through the gate.*

Danni   Well don't tell me, show me.

Michael   What's going on, what are you doing with my things Mum?

Abi   It's not working out at all Michael.

Michael   What you talkin' about?

Abi   We had an agreement, you broke it. Now I've decided . . .

Michael   You've decided? Mum these are my things!

Abi   You need help.

Michael   Help for what? Mother I truly believe you've gone over the edge this time. You went in my room again, I can't believe you went in my room.

Abi   You're moving out.

Michael   Am I?

Abi   No one is going to laugh at me any more.

Michael   Where are you getting this from please?

Abi   You're not that clever son.

Danni   That's what I told him.

Michael   Shut it.

Danni   No you shut it.

Michael   You want a slap?

Abi   Leave her alone!

Michael   Put my stuff back in my room, enough of this crap.

Abi   You promise to finish with that rubbish?

Michael   You flushed all I had down the bog.

Danni   You did that? Go Mum!

Abi   Alright Danni, quiet.

Michael   Are we finished now?

Abi   Do you promise me?

Michael   I ain't promising you shit!

Abi   Then you're going.

Michael   So what you saying Mum, you giving up on me, again?

Abi   Oh no, not this time Michael.

Michael (*laughs*)   Who you trying to fool Mum? Not me! (*Pointing at* **Danni**.) Go waste it on her. (*Grabs a box, heads back to the house.*)

Abi   I spoke to Judith this morning.

Michael   Judith! Mum Judith can fuck off . . .

Abi   Patrick's birthday next week.

Michael   So what?

Abi   She said to tell you . . .

Michael   You think I want to hear what she has to say . . .

Abi   She said to tell you, that she and David won't forget you're Patrick's father . . .

Michael   Yeah they say that now but . . .

Abi   . . . just as long as you don't! Don't you abandon him Michael.

Michael *tuts and walks back in.*

Danni *sighs. She picks up the other box.*

Abi   What are you doing? Put that down please.

Danni   He won't go Mum. He won't change.

Abi   I have.

Danni   What, you going to go through this every day?

Abi   If I have to.

Danni   You'll give up. You always do.

Abi   You really think so?

Abi *takes the box off her and tips it over.*

Danni   Alright, so what now?

Abi *laughs out loud.*

What?

Abi   How about a game of cricket?

Danni *goes back in, confused.* **Abi** *stands alone. She is still laughing. Lights up on the cricket field.* **Young Abi** *is with the team and is getting ready to bat. They both smile at each other just as* **Young Abi** *swings the bat and scores another six.*

End.

Starstruck

Starstruck was first performed at the Tricycle Theatre, London, on 19 September 1998. The cast was as follows:

Hope	Adjoa Andoh
Wally	Nigel Clauzel
Dennis	Martin Cole
Young man/Lester	George Eggay
Pammy	Hannah Lawrence
Gravel	Eddie Nestor
Little Hope	Charis Thomas/Millicent Gezy

Directed by Indhu Rubasingham
Designed by Rosa Maggiora
Lighting by Jenny Kagan
Music by Fergus O'Hare

Characters

Hope, 38
Gravel, Hope's husband
Dennis, 19, Hope's son
Little Hope, 12, Hope's daughter
Young man
Lester, a policeman
Pammy, Dennis's girlfriend
Wally, 22

The play is set in Kingston Town, Jamaica, in the 1970s.

Act One

Scene One

The Gilbey back yard. Morning. **Hope** *comes out from the house to take the washing off the line. She stops when she notices a battered old car that is in her yard.*

Hope (*furious*)   Oh Gravel! Is wat yu do now?

Kingston Bus Station. A young black man has just stepped off a bus, he enters carrying several large bags. He is struggling and looks around as if he is waiting for someone. **Dennis Gilbey** *is nearby. He watches the* **Young man** *carefully. He chooses the right time to approach him.*

Dennis   Yu awright young man?

Young man   Wat yu say?

Dennis   I ask if yu awright.

Young man   Me fine.

Dennis   Yu look like yu waitin' fer sumone.

Young man   Das my business.

Dennis   Awright man, easy nuh I juss bin friendly. Yu come down from country?

Young man   How yu know?

Dennis   Frankfield right? (**Young man** *nods.*) My mama come from Frankfield. Wat yer name? She might know yer family.

Young man   I am not givin' yu my name. My mama warned me about tief like yu . . .

Dennis   Is wat yu say man?

Young man   All yu town bwoys do is beg and tief fer money.

Dennis   Yu hear me beg yu? I don't wan' yer money.
(*Takes out some notes from his pocket.*) See it deh. I juss waiting
fer sumone like yu, he nuh here yet.

Young man   Yu don't wan' my money?

Dennis   No. Yu wan' cigarette?

Young man   Me mudda say I shouldn't smoke.

Dennis   I look like yer mudda man?

Young man *takes a cigarette,* **Dennis** *lights it for him, they enjoy
their smoke.* **Young man** *coughs a bit.*

Dennis   Yu turnin' green man.

Young man (*panics*)   A lie yu tell.

Dennis   A joke me a mek. Wa' yer name?

Young man   Adrian.

Dennis   Pleased to meet yu Adrian. William. (*They shake
hands.*) Deh yu see we not all tiefs, both our muddas come
from country, an' dat mek me a country bwoy, yu tink I
gonna tief from a country bwoy? No! So who yu waitin' fer?

Young man   My cousin Neil, 'im late.

Dennis   Neil?

Young man   Neil.

Dennis   Backside. So, it *yu* das Adrian!

Young man   Yes. Yu know me cousin?

Dennis   Yeah me know 'im. Tall right?

Young man   No man.

Dennis   Short?

Young man   No man.

Dennis   Medium height?

Young man   Yeah man.

Dennis   Yeah man me know 'im. 'Im work right?

Young man   Yeah I tink.

Dennis   Well he call me from work to say 'Dennis, go get me cousin fer me from de station ca' I have to work today'.

Young man   I tought yer name was William.

Dennis   And it is.

Young man   So why yu say yer name is Dennis?

Dennis   Dennis is my middle name, everyone call me Dennis.

Young man   So why yu tell me to call yu William?

Dennis   Adrian, calm yerself. All Neil asked me to do was put yu in a cab, mek sure yu don't get tief, ca' wat yer mudda says was right, plenty a thievin' wretches here. I not gonna tief yu. Awright, watch me now. (*Shouts.*) Cab! Over here man. See 'im comin', I go put in and mek sure 'im don't tief yu. Watch me now.

Cab driver, **Wally**, *enters.*

Wally   Who wan' de cab?

Dennis   My friend here.

Wally   Ware 'im goin'?

Young man   Taylor Street.

Wally   Me dunno ware dat is.

Dennis   Wat yu mean yu dunno?

Wally   Me dunno!

Dennis   Backside!

Wally   Yu wan' de cab or not?

Dennis   Come Adrian, show dis fool how to get deh.

Young man   My first time in Kingston.

Wally   Who wan' de cab?

Dennis   Hold on na Taylor Street, dat near Lambert's Field ain't it?

Wally   Me dunno.

Dennis   Well wat roads yu know?

Wally   Plenty!

Dennis   But not Taylor Street?

Wally   Cha me gone.

Dennis   Hold on. Wait. We're comin'. Come, Adrian, I help yu wid de bags.

Wally   Hold on a minute.

Dennis   Wat now?

Wally   Is wat yu mean 'we'?

Dennis   Two a we.

Wally   I can only tek one!

Dennis   I see yer car from here man, yu can tek two a we.

Wally   I got me tings in de back.

Dennis   Well fling yer tings out.

Wally   Look, last week my woman go throw me out.

Dennis   Come Adrian we go find another cab.

Wally   Hold on, I let yu pay half de fare. Half!

Dennis   Adrian? (**Adrian** *nods.*) Come!

Wally   Twenty dollar.

Young man   Here.

Dennis   Na man Adrian it awright. Neil give me money awready.

Dennis *gives* **Wally** *his money.*

Wally   Hey bwoy, bwoy? I say twenty dollar, not six.

Dennis   Is wat yu have in yer hand.

Wally   Six in me hand is wat me have.

Dennis   Yu can't count. (*Counts the notes.*)

Wally   Me wan' me money.

Dennis   Yer know wat happen, my gyal dis mornin' tell me she need money right, to buy food. I was in de toilet doin' my business so I juss say tek a lickle outta my wallet, de bitch mussa tek more dan half, I bet she come home wid a new dress.

Wally   Not my business if yer can't control your woman.

Dennis   At least I don't get fling out by she!

Wally   No money no cab!

Dennis   We go over to my friend Neil's. 'Im pay de rest.

Wally   Look bwoy, me I bin living on dis Island fer too long. I wan' twenty dollar. Read my lips, hear it come out, twenty dollar, twenty dollar, twenty dollar . . .

Dennis   Give de blasted man 'im money Adrian. Don't worry I tell Neil, we'll get de money back.

Wally   Right, mek up your mind who comin'.

Dennis   Adrian yu go.

Wally   Yu nuh hear de boy say 'im don't know ware de place is?

Dennis   I come wid yu first den, show you de way.

Wally   Hold on a minute.

Dennis   Wat now?

Wally   Yer gonna leave 'im here alone? What if someone come and try and tief 'im tings?

Dennis   It not far.

Young man   Maybe I can walk den.

Dennis/Wally   No!

Young man   Wat?

Dennis   Wat I mean is, it not far by car. But walking wid dem bags? No. Yu get sum good fer nuttin bwoy trying to tief it off yu, and I promise Neil I won't let nuttin 'appen to yu. Yu got room fer de bags here.

Wally   Come! (*Takes the bags and exits.*)

Young man   Hey!

Dennis   Adrian, rest yerself. (*Examines him.*) Tek your jacket off, off man! (**Adrian** *obeys, he hands it over.*) And yer tie. Now roll up yer sleeves. Unbutton de top a your shirt, show a bit a chest. Deh. Yu look like a Kingston bwoy now. Keep yer hands in yer pockets and walk around like so.

Dennis *struts around to show him.*

Dennis   Try it.

Adrian *copies* **Dennis**. *He is not as good as* **Dennis**, *who is trying very hard not to laugh.*

Dennis   Bit more strut Adrian. Swing yer hip.

Young man   Like dis.

Dennis   Yeah man.

Young man   Yu sure Kingston bwoys walk like dis?

Dennis   Alla dem. (*Car horn beeps.*) Back soon yeah. Strut Adrian strut!

Dennis *dashes off.* **Young man** *looks very confused. He is unsure what to do. He remembers the steps to strut. He begins to enjoy himself as he slowly gets the hang of it. Suddenly the penny drops.*

Young man   Police!

An alley. **Dennis** *and* **Wally** *are laughing their heads off. The* **Young man**'s *bags are emptied and contents scattered all over the* *floor.* **Dennis** *mimics the* **Young man**'s *attempts to strut; the boys laugh even more.*

Dennis   So he goes, 'yu mean like dis?'

Wally   Bwoy stupid, more stupid than dat fool fool gyal last week, remember?

Dennis (*going through the bags*)   Yu wan' mango?

Wally   Throw it here. So, how much we tek?

Dennis   Sixty dollar.

Wally   Joey's bar?

Dennis   Yeah man.

Pammy (*offstage*)   Dennis!

Wally   Jesus!

Dennis   Pammy.

Wally   Tell her to go man.

Dennis   Awright.

Pammy *enters.*

Dennis   Wa' 'appening Princess, yer awright?

Pammy   No bodder princess me right, juss no bodder.

Dennis   Rahtid, is wat me do now?

Pammy   Wat yu do? Tink Dennis, tink.

Dennis   Oh lord.

Pammy   Yes!

Dennis   I was supposed to meet yu at work right . . .

Pammy   I is not a dog Dennis.

Dennis   Pammy! Is when yu ever hear me call yu a dog?

Pammy   Don't keep me waitin' den.

Dennis Yu my princess.

Pammy And don't even bodder wid dat. Move.

Dennis Smile gyal. Look, I mek money today.

Pammy Who yu steal from now?

Dennis Look nuh, thirty dollar!

Pammy (*snatches it*) Dat can go to de fifty yu owe me awready.

Dennis Hey! We wan' go Joey's bar.

Pammy Too bad.

Wally Give de man back 'im money gyal.

Pammy Who ask yu?

Dennis Sweetiepie?

Pammy No.

Dennis Honeybuns?

Pammy No.

Dennis Yu really tink dis gonna stop me going out wid Wally?

Pammy Yes. Later.

Wally Bwoy yu juss gonna stand deh and let . . .

Dennis Hold on. (*Quotes.*) 'Oh, she doth teach the torches to burn bright! It seems she hangs upon the cheek of night.'

Wally Wat!

Pammy Stop it Dennis.

Dennis 'As a rich jewel in Ethiop's ear, beauty too rich for use for earth too dear! Did my heart love till now? Forswear it sight! For I never saw true beauty till this night.'

Pammy (*seriously aroused*) Move.

Dennis *holds her in his arms and kisses her.* **Wally** *laughs to himself, then out loud when he sees* **Dennis** *take the money out of* **Pammy***'s hand with great ease.*

Wally   Gw'n Dennis!

Dennis   Come!

Pammy   Yer wort'less wretch!

Dennis   I call yu later Pammy.

Pammy   'Bout yer tink yu can sweet talk me. Deh's plenty oder bwoys who wan' sweet talk me.

Wally   We know all about yu and dem oder bwoys Pammy.

Dennis   Wat oder bwoys?

Pammy   Tommy Riley fer one.

Dennis   Dat frog-eyed fool!

Pammy   Dat frog-eyed fool have a job, 'im have a car. He even offer to tek me to a dance on Saturday. I can call 'im any time I like.

Dennis   Well I don't like. Yu my woman Pammy Simpson.

Pammy   Yu never tek me out.

Dennis   Yu wan' go dance, I tek yu.

Pammy   Come Saturday you lose all yer money. Yu and dis fool.

Wally   Hey!

Pammy   Hey wat!

Dennis   Yu really tink I enjoy sitting down doing nuttin?

Pammy   Cha Dennis juss ferget 'bout it right. All yu do is act up and play de fool. If yu love it so much go show it to dem flim people, ca' me tired a it. Me sick an' tired a it.

Dennis Wat flim people?

Pammy Yu know man.

Dennis No.

Wally Come on Dennis, leave de gyal.

Dennis Wait nuh.

Pammy Yu really mean yu don't know?

Dennis Wat flim people Pammy?

Pammy (*acting all coy*) Nuttin.

Dennis Pammy?

Pammy It nuttin.

Dennis Pamela?

Pammy Forget it.

Dennis Wat flim? Hollywood flim?

Wally Shut up man.

Dennis It is right?

Pammy Maybe. Maybe not.

Dennis Tell me.

Pammy I tink about it.

Dennis Tell me now!

Pammy Walk wid me on de beach an' I consider it.

Dennis It have stars right?

Wally Bwoy don't beg, can't yu see dat she . . .

Dennis Pammy!

Pammy Yu go walk me to de beach? See yu later den.

Dennis (*tickles her*) Wat flim people Pamela?

Pammy   A whole heap a white people arrive in de hotel de oder day to mek sum flim.

Dennis   Ware?

Pammy   All over town. But I see sum a dem down by Lambert Street today, outside Miss Stuart's shop.

Dennis   Who star in it, yu find out? (*Goes to tickle her again.*)

Pammy   Granger!

Dennis   Granger? Stewart Granger?

Pammy   Yes!

Dennis   Jesus Christ man! Stewart Granger!

Wally   Im an actor right?

Dennis   Movie star! 'Bout actor? Dis mus' be sum big flim de mekin' if deh have 'im. Oh Pammy, it come – dis is my chance!

Wally   Wat 'im say now?

Pammy   Yu mean he nuh tell yu? Fool wan' be an actor.

Dennis   Movie star! Wait till I tell Mama.

Pammy   Deh not lookin' fer any actors man, deh got de own.

Dennis   Shut up man, deh mus wan' people to stand in de background, create the right kind a atmosphere, mek people believe deh really in Jamaica. Well, that is me, is it not?

Pammy   I tought yu knew.

Dennis   I bin busy.

Pammy   Busy tiefin'. I should kep' my mout shut.

Dennis   But such a lovely mout. Yu wan' me to get a job, I goin' get a job. I gonna be famous gyal.

Pammy   Save it fer de police.

Dennis   Why?

Pammy   Oh didn't I mention? Lester lookin' fer de two a yu.

Wally   Rass! Come on Dennis. Leave de case man.

Dennis   It made a leader! Hold it fer me Pammy.

Pammy   Oh no.

Dennis   Come on.

Pammy   I hate yu Dennis Gilbey!

They run.

The yard. **Hope** *peeling potatoes.* **Little Hope** *climbs over the fence and jumps into the yard. Her dress is torn and her face is bleeding. She tries to sneak into the house without being seen.*

Hope   Lickle Hope Gilbey!

Little Hope *freezes.*

Hope   I hope dat not yu tryin' to sneak into de house.

Little Hope   No Mama. How yu know it was me?

Hope   I got eyes in de back a my head. (*Turns round.*) Look at de state a yer dress chile. Is wat yu bin doing?

Little Hope   Nuttin.

Hope   Yu wan' fer me to get de belt?

Little Hope   No Mama.

Hope   So yu gonna tell me wat 'appen?

Little Hope   Yes Mama.

Hope   Gw'n den.

Little Hope   It was Billy Walker.

Hope   Billy Walker? 'Im a big bwoy, Lickle Hope. Wat yu doin' fighting 'im?

Little Hope   I kick 'im in de face 'im have blood all over 'im shirt.

Hope   Stop dat talk.

Little Hope   'Im call Daddy a retard.

Hope   Don't say dat word.

Little Hope   I didn't, Billy Walker say it.

Hope   Yu don't have to repeat it.

Little Hope   I tell 'im to tek it back but 'im say no.

Hope   So yu kick 'im in de face?

Little Hope   Yes. I don' wan' no one mekin' fun a Daddy.

Hope   Sure yu weren't rolling around in de dirt again?

Little Hope   It de trut Mama.

Hope   I hope so. Ca' yu an' me are gonna pay Billy's mudda a visit. And yu go say sorry, right?

Little Hope   Yes Mama.

Hope   Fighting like sum dog, yu don't feel shame? Look at yer dress.

Little Hope   Yu have to throw it away now.

Hope   Oh no. Yu gonna be wearing dis dress again, I promise yu dat. Yu pikne love to tink we got money to burn. I don't wan' to hear any more stories about yu fightin' yer hearin' me? Yu is a young lady Lickle Hope. Time fer yu to start acting like one.

Little Hope   But wat if deh start mekin' fun a Daddy . . .

Hope   It not yer concern.

Little Hope   We got a new car Mama?

Hope   No.

Little Hope   So wat it doing here?

Hope   It going right back ware it come from.

Little Hope   Has Daddy done a stupid ting again Mama?

Hope   I told yu it not yer concern.

Gravel *whistles a tune offstage.*

Little Hope (*beaming*)   It Daddy!

Hope   Gw'n inside and clean up.

Little Hope *does as she is told.* **Gravel** *enters the yard. He looks very pleased when he sees the car.*

Hope   Yu late.

Gravel   Bunch a fools carry on like dog, following de white man.

Hope   Wat yu chat 'bout now?

Gravel   Nuttin. Dinner ready?

Hope   It soon come.

Gravel   It here! It here at last Hope.

Hope   I got eyes yu nuh Gravel.

Gravel   I know wat yu gonna say.

Hope   Do yu now?

Gravel   And yu right. No way is dis ole piece a junk worth wat Ned Williams was offering. But 'im knock off half de price Hope. Half price!

Hope   Oh Gravel man!

Gravel   Gravel couldn't turn it away.

Hope   Yes 'im could.

Gravel   Our own car.

Hope   Look at de state a it.

Gravel   Yu tink he con Gravel?

Hope   Hasn't he?

Gravel   Dis my dream.

Hope   It goin' back ware it came from, and yu goin' get yer money back off Ned Williams yer hearing me?

Gravel   The car is staying right ware it is Hope, de money is staying ware it is, in Ned Williams back pocket, yu hearing me?

Hope   Yu wan' fer dem to laugh?

Gravel   No one laughin' at Gravel.

Hope   So how come yer own daughter come home with blood all over her face ca' she fighting sum bwoy who calling yu names?

Gravel   Yu tink Gravel boddered by wat a child have to say? Listen to me. (*Pitches it.*) Gravel & Son! The business. Cab business. See how full de bus get lately?

Hope   Brewster got 'im cab company down de road man.

Gravel   Brewster tell me de oder day he gettin' out. 'Im hire six drivers last month an' every one a dem run off wid 'im money.

Hope   Man love to moan, don't mean 'im ready to sell up.

Gravel   Gravel fix up de car, tek it out on de road, mek sum money, den we go out buy anudda one, do de same ting. We'll be rich!

Hope   Like we be rich having our own boat, like we be rich running our own shop . . .

Gravel   Oh shush.

Hope   Yu have a job.

Gravel   Gravel too good to be packin' bananas all 'im life.

Hope   Now yu sound like yer own son, ambition fer de young Gravel. How yu know yer can fix de damn ting.

Gravel Dis is wat Gravel meant to do.

Hope Twenty dollar say Dennis won't drive cab fer yu.

Gravel Wat dis have to do wid Dennis please?

Hope Gravel & Son?

Gravel Gravel Senior, me daddy. Dennis can find 'im own job.

Little Hope, *now dressed in T-shirt and pants, comes running out of the house.*

Little Hope Daddy!

Gravel Hey!

Hope Wat yer running fer chile?

Gravel Gravel miss dis face yu see!

Little Hope Can I play in de car Daddy?

Hope It look like toy to yu?

Gravel Gw'n.

Hope Den yu can set de table.

Little Hope *jumps in, gets behind the steering wheel and pretends to drive.*

Hope De bwoy a lot like yu nuh.

Gravel Gravel no tief.

Hope Yeah, see de worse in 'im again.

*At this point, **Dennis** climbs over the yard fence and falls over.*

Hope But Jesus Christ.

Gravel Yu were saying?

Hope Wa wrong wid yu children? Use de door!

Dennis Mama yer nuh see me right.

Hope Dennis?

Lester (*offstage*)   Gilbey!

Dennis *tries to hide in the car.*

Gravel   Oh no.

Dennis   Come on Pops.

Gravel   Out!

Dennis *dives into the chicken shed and hides.*

Little Hope (*laughing, chanting*)   Dennis in de chicken shed, Dennis in de chicken shed . . .

Hope   Quiet gyal!

Hope *shields* **Dennis** *as* **Lester** *enters.*

Lester (*out of breath*)   Yu wan' tell me ware he is?

Hope   Where's who?

Lester   Gil . . . Gilbey!

Hope   'Im not here. (**Lester** *looks around.*) Why yer can' leave 'im alone Lester?

Lester   I was chasin' 'im . . . (*Unable to say any more.*)

Hope   Oh sit down man!

Gravel (*gets a stool for* **Lester**)   Here Lester.

Hope   Yu fat . . .

Gravel   Hope!

Lester   Wat yu standin' deh fer? (*Stands up.*) Stand aside please.

Hope   Yu think I stupid enough to hide my own son in a chicken shed?

Lester   Come outta deh Gilbey.

Hope   Yu deaf?

Gravel   Awright, everyone juss calm down awright. Come Lester yu wan' to tell me wat dis is all about.

Lester   'Im and dat nephew a yours, and sum gyal. Deh got dis poor bwoy from de country, dem tek all 'im tings.

Hope   Straight away yu know it Dennis.

Lester   'Im done it before. (*Shouts at the shed.*) Yu got five seconds!

Gravel   Come Lester, we work summin out.

Lester   Wat we have to work out?

Gravel   Come see wat Gravel got, come. Come out a deh Little Hope. Wat yu tink? Lickle bit a paint,

Little Hope   I wanna paint it!

Gravel   . . . work on de engine, cab business!

Lester   Wat about Brewster?

Gravel   Brewster gone man. Look inside nuh man. Gravel gonna put nice velvet seats. Mek it look comfortable.

Lester   It gonna look good.

Gravel *takes out a bottle of rum from his tool box.*

Gravel   So anyway, how's yer daddy Lester, 'im awright?

Lester (*tempted*)   'Im fine.

Gravel   Tell 'im Gravel say how'd yu do.

Lester (*takes the bottle*)   Last time Gravel, it has to be. (*To the chicken shed.*) Yu is a lucky fool Dennis. (*Exit.*)

Gravel   Take care Lester. Yu plannin' on staying in dat shed all day?

Dennis *comes out covered in straw.*

Gravel   In all our born days, we have never had a tief in de family till yu come outta yer mudda.

Dennis   We never had anyting in all our born days!

Gravel   Not even man enough to say sorry.

Dennis (*insincere*)   Sorry.

Gravel   Lie!

Dennis   Awright me not sorry.

Gravel   See how selfish he is.

Dennis   Mek up yer mind man, wat yu wan' me to say?

Gravel   I mek up my mind an' fling yer arse out.

Hope   Gravel calm yerself.

Gravel   Yu aways defending 'im.

Hope   I'm not, I wan' yu to stay calm. (*She slaps* **Dennis** *across the head.*)

Dennis   Mama? See how deh treat me Little Hope?

Hope   No jokes.

Little Hope (*enjoying this*)   Dennis get licks!

Hope   Go inside and set de table.

Little Hope *goes inside.* **Dennis** *follows her.*

Gravel   Gravel not finish wid yu yet. Yu don't tink it time yu stop farmin' de arse wid yerself?

Dennis   Yu mean like yu? A cab business?

Gravel   Wat wrong wid dat?

Dennis (*to* **Hope**)   'Im not go learn, I tell yu awready . . .

Gravel   I ask yu a question, wat wrong wid dat? My fudda were a cab driver, my broder was a cab driver.

Dennis   Yeah, Grandaddy die old an' broke, Uncle Neville run off to Englan'.

Gravel   Maybe yu would like to fly away to Englan' den, that suit yu?

Dennis   Suited yu.

Gravel   Come juss like Neville.

Hope   Don't.

Gravel   Tief off yer own juss like de white man.

Dennis   Dem country fools not my own right, I'm my own!

Hope   I go bus' two heads in a minute.

Dennis   Yeah but . . .

Gravel   . . . An' he aways . . .

Hope   Stop.

Gravel *goes to his car.* **Hope** *walks over to him.*

Gravel   Wat yu wan'?

Hope   Ware dat bokkle a rum come from?

Gravel   It was juss a bottle, bin lyin' round.

Hope   It look like a new bottle to me. Gravel?

Gravel   Wat yu wan'?

Hope   Yu come like a blasted child. Yu know wat de doctor say . . .

Gravel   Wat de hell 'im know?

Hope   More than yu.

Gravel   Gravel go fer 'im dinner. (*Goes in.*)

Dennis (*mimics his father*)   'Wat de hell 'im know?'

Hope   Dennis?

Dennis   'Gravel go fer 'im dinner.'

Hope *clouts him around the head again.*

Dennis Mama!

Hope Enough.

Dennis Midas.

Hope (*raises her hand*)   Yer wan' anudda one? Stop calling 'im dat.

Dennis It 'appening all over again Mama.

Hope I know.

Dennis An' we're de ones dat have to sort it out.

Hope No Dennis, I'm de one dat have to sort it out.

Dennis Hey, Mama? Who win de Best Actor Oscar in 1954?

Hope I'm not in de mood.

Dennis Yu angry wid me?

Hope Yu promised me yu stop tiefing.

Dennis Wally hard up man, he need money.

Hope Is Wally go help yu when yer arse thrown in jail?

Dennis But dem country fools mek it so easy fer us, deh so stupid man. Yu shoulda seen me Mama, I was so good . . .

Hope Yu fudda come from country.

Dennis Exactly.

Hope Tek that smile right off yer face young man. I mean it. Who was de gyal?

Dennis Pammy.

Hope Is she who rope yu into dis.

Dennis Mama don't talk to me like I'm Pops, right?

Hope Yer not mekin' tings easy Dennis. I gotta deal wid yer fudda, I can't deal wid yu at de same time.

Dennis   Awright!

Hope   Bwoy yu is too good fer tiefing.

Dennis   I'm special.

Hope   Right.

Dennis   I bet I know wat can mek yu smile.

Hope   I'm not one a yer gyals yu know bwoy.

Dennis   Yu don't know.

Hope   Know wat?

Dennis   Who star in *Waterloo Road*?

Hope   Dennis!

Dennis   Who!

Hope   Stewart Granger a course. Why yu ask?

Dennis   Juss wondered.

Hope   Yu said it mek me smile. Wa' goin' on?

Dennis   Yu really wan' to know?

Hope   Yes.

Dennis   Yu sure 'bout dis?

Hope   Dennis!

Dennis   Yu best sit down den.

Hope   Yer mudda fine ware she is.

Dennis   Awright. Dinner smell good, maybe I should eat summin before . . .

Hope   So yu wan' me to beat yu?

Dennis   Awright, guess who starring in sum flim dem Hollywood people mekin' right here?

Hope   Wat?

Dennis   Come on, guess.

Hope   How de hell should I know, I didn't even know deh mekin' sum flim . . .

Dennis   Mama, yu juss said 'im name.

Hope (*not wanting to believe it*)   Shut up.

Dennis   No joke.

Hope   Yu tink me fool?

Dennis   It Pammy who tell me Mama. 'Im stayin' at de hotel ware she work. He's here.

Hope   Stewart Granger?

Dennis   Yep.

Hope   On dis island?

Dennis   Yep!

Hope (*ecstatic*)   Jesus Christ. Jesus Christ! Oh Lord, oh God . . .

Dennis   Yu wan' sit down?

Hope   Ware?

Dennis   Juss on de steps.

Hope   No yu fool, ware?

Dennis (*teasing*)   Nearby.

Hope (*like a little girl*)   Don't tease me right!

Dennis   Outside Miss Stuart's shop.

Hope   Backside! (*Runs out of the yard.*) Dennis I can't see nuttin man.

Dennis   So let's go deh.

Hope   Yes, no. Dennis go in yer fudda's shed, get me 'im binocular.

Dennis *goes.* **Hope** *climbs on the hood of the car.*

Hope (*impatient*)   Wat yu waitin' fer, rain?

Dennis (*coming out with the binoculars*)   Yu nuh answer my question yet?

Hope   Wat yu chat 'bout?

Dennis   Who win de Best Actor Oscar in 1954 . . .

Hope   Marlon Brando!

Dennis   For?

Hope   *On the Waterfront!* (*Holds out her hand for the binoculars.*)

Dennis   And who win it in 1955 . . .

Hope   Yu wan' eat in dis house?

Dennis *laughs as he throws her the binoculars. He joins her on top of the car.*

Hope   I aways knew he'd come here. Man bin all over de world mekin' flims, why shouldn't he come here?

Dennis   Well 'im here now.

Hope   Deh he is, oh my God, Stewart Granger!

Dennis (*looks through binoculars*)   Ware?

Hope (*pointing*)   Deh. Look, 'im sittin' down in 'im chair right, wid 'im sunglasses.

Dennis   Ware?

Hope   Deh bwoy, yu blind?

Dennis   No, but me can't see 'im.

Hope   'Im de only one sittin' down. Dennis, look, see how everyone else runnin' round, wid all dem lights and camera and ting?

Dennis   Yeah. Das not 'im Mama.

Hope   Yu mus' be blind. It 'im Dennis, he look de same as he did in *Beau Brummel*, tall, jet black hair . . .

Dennis   Mama, it not 'im.

Hope   Oh quiet, who ask yu anyhow?

Dennis   Awright.

Hope (*looks again*)   Yer right. It not Stewart Granger, so who it den?

Dennis   Me dunno. (*Takes the binoculars.*) Hey, who dat comin' outta de car? Raquel Welch!

Hope   Das not her Dennis.

Dennis   It look like her. She got same hair, same legs, every ting!

Hope   Close yer mout son.

Dennis   She look nice.

Hope   So ware her tits?

Dennis   Mama!

Hope   Gal ain't got no tits. Yu see dem? I see more tit on a dog. (**Dennis** *wants the binoculars.*) Move yerself.

Wally *enters the yard.*

Wally   Gilbey bwoy!

Dennis   Wa gw'n!

Wally   Hello Auntie.

Hope   Walford.

Dennis   Wally, tell Mama who dat woman is fer me please.

Wally   I dunno, but she look like Raquel Welch.

Dennis   It is Raquel Welch.

Wally   Na man.

Hope   Tank you!

Wally   Too short. All de same I wouldn't mind grind dat.

Hope   Excuse me?

Wally   I wouldn't mind actin' wid her dass wat I mean.

Hope   I know wat yu mean.

Wally   Sorry Auntie.

Dennis   Since when yu wan' act?

Wally   Well if yu wan' to do it . . .

Dennis   If deh's any part, it mine.

Wally   Deh's room fer more dan juss yu yer nuh Dennis. Or yu tink I is better dan yu?

Dennis   Yu stay which part yu deh. I go get closer, show dem wat I can do, right?

Hope   Hold on a minute. (*Brushes* **Dennis**'s *hair with her hands, and his shirt.*)

Dennis   Mama?

Hope   I don't wan yu goin' down deh, lookin' all rough.

Dennis   I go miss out.

Hope   Good luck. And hey, yu behave yerself.

Dennis   I go come back a star Mama. Hey 1962, who win Best Actor?

Hope   Gregory Peck.

Dennis (*leaving*)   Wat flim?

Hope (*calls*)   *To Kill a Mockingbird!*

Wally   So how's tings Auntie?

Hope   Fine, Walford.

Wally   Uncle Gravel angry wid me?

Hope I wouldn't stay too long if I were yu. If Dennis see Stewart Granger he better get me 'im autograph.

Wally Dat old man.

Hope Dat old man can teach yu a lot.

Wally Like wat?

Hope How to treat a woman good, mek her feel like a lady. How to talk right, stand up straight. Every ting 'im wan', 'im get.

Wally Nuttin wrong wid de way me talk.

Hope Yu island men all de same, can't see furder than yer own nosehole.

Wally 'Im juss a man like me yu know Auntie.

Hope He is a gentleman. Believe me, dis island could do wid more gentlemen.

Wally 'Im not yer type.

Hope So wat is my type den Walford?

Wally *rubs his hands up and down her thigh.* **Hope** *looks like she is enjoying it.* **Wally** *then thrusts his hand up her skirt.*

Hope Ease up nuh. Stop it! Yu wan' do it out here?

Wally Why not?

Hope Yer Uncle Gravel come out any minute, yu mad?

Wally Yu like living dangerously.

Hope No!

Wally I nuh see yu fer weeks.

Hope Yu get too crazy Walford.

Wally Auntie, yu mek me crazy.

Hope Stop! (*Climbs down.*)

Wally Come round de corner.

Hope   I look like whore to yu?

Wally   One minute.

Hope   I haven't got a minute. Gravel only inside man.

Wally   Leave 'im, leave wid 'im toy.

Hope   Wat yu mean by dat? Walford?

Wally   I bump into Ned, he tell how much Gravel pay fer dis. (*Laughs.*)

Hope   It not funny.

Wally   Everyting dat fool do is funny. Ned bin trying to get rid a dis fer months. No one would touch it, 'cept Gravel. Hey come on.

Hope   I don't wan' yu.

Wally   Oh man, don't play dis game again.

Hope   I'm not playing. Yu not gettin' nuttin outta me Walford till yu tell yer friend Ned I go be callin' on 'im.

Wally   Not even a feel?

Hope   No.

Wally   Suck on yer tittie?

Hope   Juss tell 'im I wan' 'im to buy de car back.

Wally   Yu mus be jokin'!

Hope   My face tell yu I jokin'? I wan' 'im to pay double wat Gravel give 'im. (**Wally** *laughs.*) So he can mek up any story he like, so long as he mek it good.

Wally   Ned won't go fer dat.

Hope   Ned have no choice.

Wally   Wat yu mean?

Hope   Let's juss say 'im wife wouldn't like it.

Wally   Yu sleeping wid 'im?

Hope   And wat if I were?

Wally   I wouldn't like it.

Hope   Yu don't own me Wally. No one own me. I'm not sleeping wid 'im. But me know who is.

Wally   Who?

Hope   Dat fer me to know, and 'im wife to find out if he don't play ball.

Wally   All dis fer Gravel Gilbey.

Hope   No one cons my husband and gets away wid it right? I'm sick a everyone laughin' at 'im.

Wally   Awright. But wat in it fer me?

Hope   Soon Walford.

Wally   Yu wan' drive me mad?

Hope   Calm yerself. Jesus! Lickle bit a fun an' yu get all excited.

Wally   Come away wid me.

Hope   Yu don't listen.

Wally   We go live in Spanish Town yeah?

Hope   Yu really do that?

Wally   I'd do any ting fer yu.

Hope   Stop talkin' like a fool Wally.

Wally   My fault me love yu?

Hope   Yu love me? Bwoy yu nuh tink I never hear dat before?

Wally   I mean it.

Hope   Say it again den.

Wally   I love yu Hope.

Hope   Say 'yer the only ting worth stayin' fer on dis island, Hope Kiffin'.

Wally   Yer the only ting worth stayin' fer on dis island, Hope Kiffin.

Hope *shakes her head.*

Wally   Who was I supposed to be?

Hope   No mind.

Wally   Who?

Hope   Juss tell everyone to leave my husban' alone right? 'Im not lazy like yu, 'im have a job.

Wally   Had a job, 'im a leave.

Hope   No, 'im only say he going to leave.

Wally   'Im a leave. Yu know Thurston who work wid 'im right? I hear 'im say Uncle and de boss a dat factory have a big argument. Boss say 'im pack box wrong, Gravel call 'im an ejut – right in front a everybody.

Hope (*angry*)   Gravel!

Wally   He nuh even tell 'im own wife de trut.

Hope (*snaps*)   Every day it summin, every blasted day it aways summin!

Wally   Ease up.

Hope   I don't wan' to ease up. I juss wan' . . .

Wally   Wat?

Hope   Never mind.

Wally   Tek yer mind off tings fer a minute. Relax, have sum fun. Den I tell Ned, I promise yu. Feel my ting. Feel it.

Gravel *comes out of the house. He sees them.*

Hope   It gettin' big. No Wally wait, wait! Come round corner.

Hope *and* **Wally** *disappear behind the yard fence.* **Gravel** *watches them leave. He goes over to his car and lifts up the bonnet.*

Gravel   Watch me now, Pops.

Scene Two

The next day. **Dennis** *and* **Pammy** *are in the yard.*

Dennis   '. . . She speaks. Yet she says nothing. What of that? Her eye discourses. I will answer it. I am too bold, 'tis not to me she speaks. Two of the fairest stars in all the heaven, having some business, do entreat her eyes to twinkle in their spheres till they return. What if her eyes were there, they in her head? The brightness of her cheek would shame those stars as daylight doth a lamp.' (*To* **Pammy**.) Excited?

Pammy   Maybe.

Dennis   Yu wan' come inside?

Pammy   No.

Dennis   All me ever hear from yu is no.

Pammy   An' yu go go on hearing it.

Dennis   We go marry anyway.

Pammy   I nuh see no ring on my finger.

Dennis   Yu know we go do it?

Pammy   When?

Dennis   Soon. So we might as well, yu know.

Pammy   No.

Dennis   I can't remember de las time I have de house to myself. I know yu wan' to. I can tell.

Pammy   Oh yes?

Dennis   'Her eyes in heaven would through the airy region stream so bright that birds would sing and think it were not right. See how she leans her cheek upon her hand! Oh that I were a glove upon her hand! That I might touch that cheek!'

Pammy   Nuttin but rubbish!

Dennis   Rubbish? Dis is Shakespeare gyal. Romeo pouring out 'im heart to Juliet, only gyal 'im love in de whole world, fool dead fer her. It romance. Yu don't wan' romance Pammy?

Pammy   Oh I wan' it.

Dennis (*glad*)   Good.

Pammy   Togeder with marriage, house, and pikne.

Dennis   Maybe I should go check yer mudda. I bet she coulda mek me happy.

Pammy *kicks him hard.*

Dennis   Ow! Easy nuh Pammy.

Pammy   Don't tell me 'bout easy.

Dennis   Will yu stop kicking me, please?

Pammy   Yu wan' my mama so bad? Go den. She at home waitin' fer yu, and de rest of a whole line a men wid thirty dollar in deh pocket . . . Go if das wat yer . . . (**Dennis** *grabs her foot just as she tries to kick him again.*) Let go a my foot.

Dennis   Yer mean dis foot?

Pammy   Let go.

Dennis (*strokes her foot*)   Skin smooth. (*Sniffs.*) Feet stink!

Pammy   I hate yu!

Dennis   No yu don'.

Pammy   Yu mek me sick.

Dennis   Yu love me, yu can't stop dreamin' about me.

Pammy   Let me go now!

Dennis   Calm down. I was juss tryin' to mek yu jealous like yu did wid me when yu say Tommy Riley wan'ed to . . .

Pammy   Forget Tommy Riley. Yu really tink I coulda interest in dat frog-eyed fool? Nuh smile at me.

Dennis   I love yu Pammy.

Pammy   Yeah, when yer wan' summin. Yu don't wan fer marry me.

Dennis   Who say I don't?

Pammy   Yu nuh even find job yet.

Dennis   I'm workin' on it. It my fault dem flim people tell me de don' wan' me?

Pammy   Shut up about de flim man.

Dennis   I can act, Pammy.

Pammy   Dem never tink so.

Dennis   Dem never give a chance, all dem say is 'move'.

Pammy   I don't wan' to be married to an actor, hear me now, I wan' be married to a man dat go look after me.

Dennis   I can do both. Yu an' me are go live in a big house, Pammy Simpson. I tellin' yu.

Pammy   And in de mean time?

Dennis   I dunno Pammy.

Pammy (*mimics*)   I dunno Pammy!

Dennis   Wat yer have to ruin de dream fer?

Pammy   Ca' yu can't live on dreams.

Dennis   But wat if yu could? Wat if all yu had to do snap yer fingers, and watever yu wan', yu get. Yu tellin' me de world wouldn't be a better place if dat were so?

Pammy   I dunno Dennis.

Dennis (*mimics*)   I dunno Dennis.

Pammy   Dreams are in yer head fool, ware deh supposed to be. Stop playin' de arse and go back to work.

Dennis   Too late. Factory job gone.

Pammy   Work fer yer pops den.

Dennis   Work fer Midas? Everything 'im touch turn to shit.

Pammy   I tink it a good idea. Yu see how full de bus get lately?

Dennis   Two months me give 'im.

Pammy   Don't mek fun a 'im.

Dennis   It all I can do. I can't yell at de man in case 'im get all work up and have anudda heart attack. It my fault 'im sick, 'im aways sick.

Pammy   Yu don't know how lucky yu are, havin' a fudda.

Dennis   Sorry Mama.

Pammy   I wish I was yu nuh, give yu two licks in yer head.

Dennis   I not askin' Midas fer nuttin Pammy.

Pammy   It go kill yu?

Dennis   Yu are so good ain't it, wan' to look after everybody, Pammy Simpson.

Pammy   Yu wait till we marry. Gonna put yu under serious manners. Dennis Gilbey.

Dennis (*aroused*)   Can' wait.

Pammy   Best speak to yer fudda den.

Dennis   Awright. But yu can't do a lickle summin fer me now?

Pammy *undoes the top buttons on her blouse.*

Pammy   Juss a feel.

Dennis *puts his hands down* **Pammy**'s *blouse.* **Pammy** *moves her head as* **Dennis** *tries to kiss her.*

Dennis   Tiny lickle kiss?

Pammy *lets him kiss her.* **Little Hope** *enters, carrying bags of shopping. She giggles to herself as she watches* **Dennis** *and* **Pammy**.

Little Hope   Gw'n Dennis!

Dennis *and* **Pammy** *look up.*

Dennis   Little Hope!

Little Hope   I know wat yu bin doin'.

Dennis   No yu don't.

Little Hope   Grindin'! (*Thrusts her pelvis back and forth.*)

Dennis   Lickle scamp, come here!

Little Hope (*chanting*)   No! Dennis grindin' Pammy, Dennis grindin' Pammy . . .

Dennis   Come here before, I go gobble yu all up!

Little Hope (*still laughing*)   No!

Dennis *chases his sister into the house.* **Hope** *enters the yard carrying bags of shopping.*

Hope   Wass all de blasted noise in here? (*Clocks* **Pammy**.)

Pammy (*cold*)   Mrs Gilbey.

Hope (*even colder*)   Pamela.

Pammy   Yu wan' help wid those?

Hope   I can manage. (*Sees the shopping* **Little Hope** *has put on the ground.*) Lickle Hope? Why yu nuh put de shopping away like I tell yu to? (*Shouts.*) Lickle Hope?

Pammy   She not across de street yu nuh.

Hope (*shouting again*)   Little Hope!

Little Hope *runs out chased by* **Dennis**.

Hope   Little Hope, don't mek me chase yu. Tek de shopping inside like me tell yu to. Dennis help yer sister. (*They go in.*) Bwoy how old are yu? Carrying on like yu six.

Pammy   I tink he still is.

Hope   So, yu still following my son around huh Pamela?

Pammy   I don' follow no one around.

Hope   Yu sleep wid 'im yet?

Pammy   Pardon?

Hope   Have you slept wid my son yet?

Pammy   Das none a yer business.

Hope   Juss hurry up, right, an' give 'im wat he wan', ca' if it money yu after . . .

Pammy   I don't wan' money.

Hope   . . . He nuh have none. It juss me and 'im fudda lookin' after 'im . . .

Pammy   Yu turn deaf?

Hope   Give wat 'im wan', and go.

Pammy   Yu don' know wat 'im wan'. Yu tink you do, yer spoil 'im rotten but yer don'.

Hope   My son nineteen years old. Wat yu tink is on de minds a bwoys 'im age? Yu go tell me I wrong now? It nuttin personal sweetheart.

Pammy Yes it is. Everything yer say to me is personal. Ca' we both know if my name were anything but Simpson yu wouldn't be talkin' to me dis way. I here co' I wan' to be right.

Hope Mout like yer tramp mudda.

Pammy Comin' from yu das a compliment.

Hope I juss counting de days when he finally get sick a yu.

Pammy Dat won't happen.

Hope It will, soon as yu open yer legs.

Pammy Den I won't open my legs.

Hope Yu be tellin' me yu virgin next Pamela.

Pammy Yu not mekin' me upset again. How's Wally Mrs Gilbey? Yer nephew?

Hope Me know who he is.

Pammy I haven't seen 'im fer a while.

Hope Yu know dam well yu, he and Dennis were by de bus station yesterday.

Pammy Oh yes. We went Joey's bar. Wally love a drink yu know. Bwoy 'im can talk.

Hope Listen right, my son don't wan' yu, he wan' dat! (*Points at* **Pammy**'s *crotch*.)

Hope *goes inside.* **Gravel** *enters the yard, whistling the same tune he did before. He is holding a brand new steering wheel.*

Gravel Hey Pammy!

Pammy Oh hi Mr Gilbey.

Gravel Gravel! Me name Gravel chile, how many more times?

Pammy Sorry.

Gravel   Hey, na, na, na, na, no long faces in dis yard, nossir! Now ware dat smile Pammy have, de one Gravel love? Ware it deh? Ware it deh?

Pammy *laughs.*

Gravel   Yes! Tank yu! Yer face could light up a room, Pammy Simpson.

Pammy   Yu aways say dat.

Gravel   Ca' it true, and Gravel aways speak de trut. Wat Hope bin sayin' to yu now?

Pammy   I don' care wat she say to me.

Gravel   It Dennis she should be yellin' at, not yu.

Pammy   She tell me dat he don't love me, he only after one ting. It not true is it?

Gravel   Course not chile, bwoy crazy 'bout yu. 'Im inside too? (**Pammy** *nods.*) Good!

Gravel *takes a secret swig from his flask.*

Gravel   Right! Gravel go work!

Pammy   Yu get it goin' yet? (**Gravel** *gets in the car and turns on the engine; it is still choking.*) Don' like dat.

Gravel   But it a start right. Gravel soon get her worried. 'Im tell her whom boss.

Pammy   I do love Dennis yu nuh Gravel. 'Im de only bwoy dat mek me laugh.

Gravel   'Im mek me mad.

Pammy   But 'im aways goes on about wat 'im wan', never wat 'im have. Now he wan' be in dat flim.

Gravel   Yes. Stewart Granger, de hero.

Pammy   De fool. Man can' even act. Wid 'im long face.

Gravel   An' 'im big nose.

Pammy   An' 'im old, wid 'im grey hair. Dennis wan' be like dat?

Gravel   Dennis fool, Pammy. 'Im dream too much.

Pammy   Das wat 'im say about yu.

Gravel   'Im can say wat 'im like. Hollywood! Superstar! 'Im and 'im mudda ferget, right? Gravel live in de white man world, 'im know wat it like, but deh nuh listen. Nossir. Gravel ever tell yu, 'im daddy was de best cab driver in Kingston? Quick time he get yu from A to B! Soon everybody talk 'bout me same way. Soon, Pammy. Deh all change de mind, Dennis too.

Pammy   Mek way we change it fer 'im den.

Gravel   How?

Pammy   When he come askin' fer a job, give it to 'im.

Gravel   Dennis go ask me?

Pammy   He promised.

Gravel   De only promise dat bwoy ever mek was never keep a promise.

Pammy   Dis time he promised his fiancée.

Gravel   Wat?

Pammy   Don't get upset.

Gravel   Fiancée?

Pammy   Dennis an' me juss wan'ed to keep it quiet fer a lickle while, we wan'ed to surprise yer both.

Gravel   Marriage, Pammy, to 'im! Yu sure 'bout dis?

Pammy   Yu juss say 'im mad about me.

Gravel   But 'im a bwoy dough Pammy.

Hope *comes out of the house, carrying a small bottle of pills and a glass of water.*

Hope Gravel?

Gravel Wat!

Hope Come on.

Gravel I look like a baby?

Hope Don't act like one.

Gravel Pammy, Gravel look sick to yu?

Pammy Nossir!

Gravel See, yu hear dat?

Hope Juss come on.

Gravel *takes the pill and water. He burps. He and* **Pammy** *laugh.*

Hope Yu drinkin' again? (**Gravel** *sucks his teeth.*) Fine. Yu juss carry on deh Gravel.

Gravel Gravel busy.

Pammy My mudda say deh's nuttin more nice dan seein' a man hard at work.

Gravel Das right.

Hope And man wid money.

Gravel Awright Hope.

Pammy I gone.

Gravel (*calls*) Dennis!

Pammy Na it awright.

Gravel I'll get 'im chile, Dennis!

Pammy Tell 'im I see 'im later.

Hope Let her go Gravel. She muss have friends to meet, right Pamela?

Pammy Right. How's yer nephew Wally, Gravel?

Gravel   Im fine.

Pammy   Tell 'im I say hello right . . . I gone (*Exit.*)

Gravel *gives* **Hope** *a look.*

Hope   Wat? Look Gravel dat sweet gyal act nuh fool me right.

Gravel   Pammy not like her mudda.

Hope   Whu yu aways believe her?

Gravel   Ca' Pammy nuh lie. Why she ask after Walford when she see 'im all de time?

Hope   Me dunno. Who know wat go on in de gyal head?

Dennis *comes into the yard. He has* **Little Hope** *on his shoulders.*

Dennis (*announces*)   Tonight's menu. Lickle Hope soup!

Little Hope   No!

Dennis   Yes!

Gravel   Put yer sister down and come over here.

Little Hope   Don't shout at 'im.

Hope   Inside, Lickle Hope.

Little Hope *runs back in.*

Gravel   Wat dis marriage business wid yu and Pammy?

Hope   Wat!

Dennis   I not go marry Pammy, Mama.

Gravel   Not wat she tink.

Dennis   I know.

Gravel   So wat yu go do?

Dennis   I don't know.

Gravel   Well yu better find out.

Dennis   Look, I like de girl Pops, but she wan' marry me. She mekin' all kind a plans. I try tell her, but she nuh listen.

Gravel   Bwoy don't play wid me.

Dennis   I not playin' wid yu Pops.

Gravel   Yer playin' wid me.

Dennis   Yu wan' me to marry her den?

Gravel   Wid wat, yu have no money.

Dennis   I know dat.

Gravel   Yu have no job.

Dennis   I know dat too.

Gravel   Lord knows wat a nice gyal like dat see in yu. She deserve better.

Hope   A Simpson.

Gravel   She a human being, Hope.

Hope   Oh yes?

Gravel   An' deh feel, deh hurt. Yu hearin' me Dennis?

Dennis   Is whole street can hear yu.

Gravel   Are yu hearin' me!

Dennis   Why yu aways have to look at me wid dat long face a yours? It kill yu to smile? Try it it easy, yu juss move yer mout like so . . .

Gravel   Don' joke wid me Dennis. Gravel tell yu awreddy 'im don' like it. Yu tell dat gyal how yu really feel right, or Gravel will.

Dennis   Fine.

Gravel   Well?

Dennis   Yu wan' me to go now?

Gravel   Right now.

Dennis   I gone.

Gravel   She also say yu wan' to help me wid de cab. Dat a lie too?

Dennis   Yu tell me.

Gravel   Don't matter, ca' yu workin' wid me.

Dennis   Come on Pops, wat I know about cars?

Gravel   Gravel teach yu.

Dennis   An' wat yu know?

Gravel   Everyting my Daddy teach me.

Dennis   Mama?

Hope   Don't look at me son.

Gravel   Yu wan' stop tinkin' wid dat. (*Points to his own crotch.*)

Dennis   Tanks but I got my own ting.

Gravel   Every ting a nasty joke to yu.

Dennis   Least me know how to joke. An' yu mad if yer tink I go waste my life drivin' cab.

Gravel   Yer wan' live in my house? Eat my food? From now on yu stay ware Gravel keep 'im eye on yu, no more tiefing, no more watchin' dat fool Stewart Granger.

Hope   Stewart Granger no fool.

Gravel (*sees* **Dennis** *is still there*)   Yu still here?

Dennis   Yu still talkin'.

Gravel   Go see Pammy.

Dennis   I will if yu let me.

Gravel   Gravel not stoppin' yu.

Dennis   Yu still talkin' to me.

Gravel   I am not.

Dennis   Yu are Pops.

Gravel   I am not . . .

Dennis   Yer are . . .

Hope   Dennis, juss go.

Dennis *exits.*

Gravel   I suppose yu tink Gravel doing de wrong ting again?

Hope   Me nuh say a word.

Gravel   Yu encourage 'im.

Hope   I do not.

Gravel   Fillin' up 'im head, tellin' 'im he can do wat he wan'.

Hope   Im can do wat 'im wan'. 'Im can do any ting, yu don' know yer own son by now? And Dennis wouldn't be de way he was wid dat gyal, if gyals like dat didn't lie down on deh back. Dat Pammy Simpson, she have yu fooled.

Gravel   Nobody have Gravel fooled.

Hope   Oh, an' I suppose Ned Williams isn't laughing behind yer back right now?

Gravel   No an' yer know why? Ca' only dis mornin' right, 'im offer to buy de car back: twice more dan wat Gravel pay.

Hope   And yu say no.

Gravel   Of course me say no. Ned worried, 'im know Gravel can do it, he probably bin tinking about starting up a cab business imself.

Hope   Well it better work dis time. Ca' me sewing dresses is not enough to feed us all. (*Puts her arm round him.*) Gravel.

Gravel   Wat yu doin'?

Hope   Oh shush man.

Gravel   Gravel wan' work, Hope.

Hope   Car not going any place. Yu allowed to hold me as well yer nuh, Gravel.

Gravel *feels awkward with this show of emotion from* **Hope**. *He is unsure what to do.*

Hope   I know wat yu tinkin'.

Gravel   Do yu?

Hope   Im a young man now.

Gravel   Das wat frighten me.

Hope   He wan' to live 'im own life.

Gravel   Don't mean he have to hurt dat girl right! He don' have to hurt anybody.

Hope   Why yu angry wid me?

Gravel   Gravel not angry.

Hope   Yu aways angry. Why yu ever get angry wid dem?

Gravel   Gravel don' care . . .

Hope   . . . wat dem tink. Well 'im should. Ca' it me, yer son and yer daughter, de ones dat have to stand up to dem. Yu tink any one a dem care about yu de way we do?

Gravel   I don' wan' yu to care.

Hope   Wat den?

Gravel *holds his wife. He kisses her.*

Hope   Awright man, juss go easy yeah?

Gravel *pulls away from her.*

Hope   All me say . . .

Gravel   Yu tink Gravel weak, Gravel not weak right, Gravel strong, Gravel strong right, 'im strong.

Gravel *runs round the yard.*

Hope   Gravel stop it, stop it man!

Gravel   Gravel strong.

Hope   Awright enough yeah? Stop it.

Gravel *gets on the ground and does sit-ups.*

Hope (*pleading*)   Gravel!

Gravel *pushes* **Hope** *away as she tries to stop him.*

Hope   For God's sake nuh man. Wa wrong wid yu?

Gravel   Gravel strong, Gravel strong, Gravel strong . . .

Hope   Yu wan' kill yerself? Yu wan' kill yerself Gravel, well go ahead! (*Goes back in the house.*)

Gravel   Gravel strong, Gravel strong, Gravel . . . (*Breaks down in tears.*)

Scene Three

Next day in the yard. **Dennis** *and* **Wally** *are sitting on top of the car watching the film being made.* **Wally** *has the binoculars.*

Wally (*turned on*)   Man who is dat woman? She look nice. I wonder if dis movie an X we might see her tittie or summin. Yu ever see a white woman's tittie?

Dennis   Nearly.

Wally   Is wat yu mean 'nearly'?

Dennis   When I was lickle Mama took me to see *Dr No*, James Bond and 'im gal, Honey Ryder, dem get caught an' deh have to go through a shower ca' de get radiation, an' fer lickle second right, yu can see bit a de gal tittie. Nice.

Wally   Real life Dennis, not de movies.

Dennis   It was real life. Dat was her real tittie I saw, I don't think we were supposed to see it, musta bin a mistake deh mek . . .

Wally   Awright, have yu ever see a white woman tittie outside de cinema?

Dennis   No.

Wally   Tank you. *Dr No*! Yu carry on like yer pops sumtimes.

Dennis   Yer ever see a white woman tittie den?

Wally   Last summer when I was working in de hotel. I had to bring a drink to sum white woman lying on de beach. She lift up her head right, an' her bikini top drop down, boom, me see dem! She look nice too. And yer know wat, she smile at me. She tell me to go jump her right deh.

Dennis   Lie.

Wally   It trut. Dem white women love de black man. Deh feel no shame, too. Broad daylight me have her!

Dennis   Yu lie man.

Wally   Well wat yu know, bwoy! Yu nuh even grind yer gal yet. If dat were me right, me woulda had her from time! Wa' wrong wid yu? She a Simpson gyal Dennis, she easy, she ripe. If yer can't grind dat yu be a batayman.

Dennis   How yu know me nuh grind her awready?

Wally   Ca' yu woulda said. Ca' I can aways tell when yu lie. Yu grind her Dennis, have yu, have yu? Have yu, have yu . . .

Dennis   No! I wan' grind her so bad, my ting get hard, it feel like it go brok off.

Wally   Batayman!

Dennis   Maybe I should marry her.

Wally   Yer mad! Listen right, marriage ain't nuttin but a bad word. Yu see me, no woman go trap me.

Dennis   Wat 'bout dat married woman yu messin' wid? I see de way yu look when yu chat 'bout her.

Wally   Me nuh love her. Only oder day right, she beg me to tek her round corner. I said to her 'Na woman. Wally got tings to do, people to see', but she on her hands and knees. So I did, keep her quiet yer know. She stuck on me man, way Wally like it.

Dennis   Min' her husband.

Wally   Man a jack arse. Fool don't deserve woman like dat.

Dennis   See? Yu love her man.

Wally   Shut up man, cha yer wan' to marry Pammy go ahead. I bored. Let's go to de bus station.

Dennis   Hold on. Deh look, deh's Granger. I wish Mama was here.

Wally   Come on man.

Dennis   Wait.

Dennis *sees something. He laughs out.*

Wally (*takes the binoculars*)   Nuh man!

Dennis   Gw'n Granger.

Wally   If dat were real life, no way could a old man like dat beat up six young man. See dat bwoy over deh, holdin' Granger by de neck? Who 'im look like to yu?

Dennis   Manny Christie! How de hell he get a part in de flim? He can't act.

Wally   Im don't need to act, juss fight.

Dennis (*yelling*)   Yu ugly wretch Manny!

Wally   Im getting eighty dollars to be ugly.

Dennis   Come on Granger, tump 'im!

Wally   Bus station?

Dennis   Hold on a minute. Manny lying on de floor now, summin happened. Look like he broke 'im leg or summin.

Wally   Obeah man!

Dennis   Watch me now.

Wally   Deh fling you out awready.

Dennis   I juss go stand near. I de same shape as Manny, deh soon spot me.

Wally   Yer askin' fer trouble Dennis.

Dennis   I go come back a star Wally! Watch me now . . .

Dennis *loses his balance and falls off the car.* **Wally** *laughs out loud.*

Act Two

Scene One

Back yard. A week later. **Hope** *is sitting down sewing a dress.*
Gravel *is in the car. He turns on the engine. It is still choking.*
Hope *looks at him.*

Gravel   Wat? (*Goes inside.*)

Dennis *bursts into the yard. He is dressed in a very smart expensive new suit. He strolls in singing along to the James Bond theme tune.*

Dennis (*in a Sean Connery accent*)   You are looking very delicious tonight, Miss Moneypenny.

Hope   Not a brass farding.

Dennis   Money! Dear mother I do not require money.

Hope (*amazed*)   Oh my Lord! Is dis my son?

Dennis   Smart, right?

Hope   How much it cost?

Dennis   Enough. Yer shoulda seen me walk right into dat shop, put me money down, and say, me wan' dat suit, gimme it! (*Sniffs.*) I love de smell a a new suit.

Hope (*sniffing the suit as well*)   Dennis man, yu smell good!

Dennis   Told yu I'd come back a star Mama.

Hope   De give yu more to do in de flim?

Dennis   Yes, no more crowd scenes fer me. De director pick me out imself to start up a bar fight wid Granger.

Hope   Yu start up a bar fight wid Granger?

Dennis   Yeah man.

Hope   So wat happen?

Dennis   I fling a bokkle at Granger's head, he hit me wid 'im chair, next ting whole bar break out in a fight. After dat right, de director come over, 'im tap me on de shoulder and 'im say, 'Well done'.

Hope (*so proud*)   Oh Dennis!

Dennis   Close yer eyes Mama.

Hope   Why?

Dennis   Juss close dem.

Hope   Lord Jesus, why yu love to tease me so?

Dennis *disappears through the yard door, he comes back a second later, holding an A4 size photograph.*

Dennis   Keep dem closed.

Hope   Dem closed.

Dennis   Now hold out yer hands.

Hope   Wat yu got fer me?

Dennis *places the photograph on her hands.*

Dennis   Open!

Hope *opens her eyes. She sees what* **Dennis** *has given her.*

Hope   But Jesus Christ!

Dennis   Tell yu I get yu it.

Hope (*reading*)   'To Hope Gilbey, my No.1 fan. Love and best wishes from Stewart Granger.' (*Thrilled.*) Thank yu. Oh my . . . how de hell yu get dis?

Dennis   I ask 'im fer it.

Hope   Yu say yu can hardly get near im, when yer get near im?

Dennis   It happen by accident. I was juss walking along, tekin' a break, an' I juss see im, sitting in 'im own chair, reading 'im paper – alone dis time. He aways before had big hefty people watchin' over im, movin' us away from 'im. So I juss tell myself, 'Do it Dennis'. I tek a deep breath, walk straight over to 'im . . .

Hope (*eager*)   Yes?

Dennis   I said, Wa' 'appenin'? I'm Dennis Gilbey.

Hope   Wa' appenin'?

Dennis   Yeah.

Hope   Yu say 'wa' 'appenin'' to Stewart Granger? 'Im a Hollywood superstar Dennis, he come from Englan'. You know how posh dem talk, yu can't say tings like 'wa' 'appenin' to 'im.

Dennis   Mama he didn't mind, 'im nice.

Hope   So wat 'im say?

Dennis (*putting on a posh English accent*)   'How do you do?'

Hope (*dreamy*)   'How do you do.' Wat else?

Dennis   He tought I was really good beating 'im up an' dat, so I says, 'Well I tink yer really good too, Mr Granger, pretendin' yer young when yu really old.'

Hope   Yu didn't? Dennis!

Dennis   Im laugh. He is old now though Mama, I see 'im face real close, 'im have a whole heap a wrinkles.

Hope   Im aways be young to me. Wat else?

Dennis   Das it. His people come back and pushed me away from im, but not before I got yu dat, an' told 'im all about yu. How yu seen all 'im flims since when yu were lickle, how yu tek me to see dem.

Hope (*thrilled*)   He ask yu wat my favourite one was?

Dennis   *Prisoner of Zenda*!

Dennis *grabs one of his father's spanners. He waves it about, pretending it is a sword.*

Dennis   Deh going back to England soon, finish de movie. Yu know wat, maybe he might speak to de director and get me a bigger part in de flim. Deh might tek me back to England wid dem. Granger like me Mama.

Hope   Course 'im like yu, why shouldn't he like yu? Yu is a good actor bwoy.

Dennis   Can't wait to see de look on Pammy's face.

Hope   I tought yu tell de gyal to clear off.

Dennis   Not yet. Soon Mama.

Hope   I know all about yer soons. Deh don' come till next year. Yu got more important tings to do now than go chasin' after dat slut.

Dennis   I tell her.

Hope   Yu better.

Dennis   I will. Yu like yer present?

Hope   Course me like it. (*Admires her picture.*) I go have to buy a nice frame fer dis man, put it up in de living room. (*In love.*) Stewart Granger!

Dennis   How old was Stewart Granger when 'im mek *King Solomon's Mines*?

Hope   Thirty-six.

Dennis   Wat year it come out?

Hope   1949.

Dennis   Who win Best Actor Oscar in 1956?

Hope   Yul Brynner.

Dennis   Wat flim?

Hope   *King an' I.*

Dennis   Who starred wid Humphrey Bogart in *Sabrina Fair*?

Hope   William Holden, Audrey Hepburn.

Dennis   Wat year Dennis Gilbey win 'im first Oscar? What year 'im marry Natalie Wood?

Hope   Oh so it she now?

Dennis   When I rich and famous, how many house yu wan'?

Hope   Just de one darling.

Dennis   I buy Lickle Hope a boat, and twenty-odd cars fer Pops to fix up.

Hope   We'll hardly see 'im den. Buy 'im a hundred.

Dennis   How come yu never tek 'im to see a Stewart Granger flim Mama?

Hope   Gravel more a a Gary Cooper man. Me an' yer Uncle Neville de ones who love Granger. Every time a new flim come, we first in de queue. Going to de movies wid 'im was fun man.

Dennis   Maybe yu shoulda married 'im den. Yu is a good looking woman yer nuh, Mama.

Hope   Tank yu kind sir.

Dennis   Musta had plenty men running after yu.

Hope   Dennis Gilbey wat yu trying to say?

Dennis   Why yu choose Pops?

Hope   Don't speak about yer fudda so, Dennis.

Dennis   All yer life yu wan' to sew dress?

Hope   Im a wonderful man.

Dennis   Wat 'im ever done tha' bin wonderful?

Hope   He left England to be wid me.

Dennis   But ho shoulda married you deh. I wouda bin born deh. Imagine de kinda life we coulda had.

Hope   Yu know how old yer fudda was when I first met im? Eleven. I musta bin 'bout seven. Guess wat 'im doing? Tap dancin' outside Joey's bar fer money. He was good. Everybody watchin' dis lickle country bwoy wid 'im fancy steps. He mek good money, but nobody watchin' 'im lickle friend Bernie tekin' deh wallet and money outta all deh pockets.

Dennis (*laughs*)   Gravel Gilbey!

Hope   Yes.

Dennis   Scam fer money?

Hope   When I saw dat man, I knew dat was a bwoy I could have fun with.

Dennis   So wat happened to 'im den?

Hope   Nuttin.

Dennis   Oh come on.

Hope   Im still dat bwoy Dennis, yu juss mus look fer it.

Gravel *comes out.*

Dennis   Hey Pops!

Dennis *tries to tap dance, he extends his hand to* **Gravel**, *inviting him to join in.*

Gravel (*unimpressed*)   Yu fall sumware on yer head?

Dennis   No.

Gravel (*takes the spanner off* **Dennis**)   Dis look like toy to yu?

Dennis   Like my suit Pops?

Gravel   Ware yu tief it? I hope yu givin' yer mudda money.

Dennis (*taking out a wad of notes, gives* **Hope** *some*)   Here you are Mother, buy yourself something ever so nice out a that.

Gravel   Oh yes we de big man now don't it?

Dennis   An' yu hate dat don't it?

Gravel   Tell me summin. Wat yu go do when de flim finish? Tiefin'? Ca' if yu are, let me tell yu summin right . . .

Dennis   I don't tief no more.

Gravel   So wat yu go do?

Dennis   If yu mus know, I go to Englan', I go act.

Gravel   Yu go England? (*Laughs.*) Yu wouldn't last two days.

Dennis   Yu lasted two years.

Gravel   Juss ca' deh give yu a lickle bit a money to farm de fool Dennis . . .

Dennis   I not farmin' de fool! Come on Pops, yer son get beaten up by Stewart Granger.

Gravel   Old man like 'im.

Hope   Im not dat old.

Gravel   Im old.

Dennis   It an important scene, de man playing my boss has kidnapped Granger's wife, so he come out here to rescue her, but den she and de man . . .

Gravel   Gravel don't wan' to hear none a yer stupidness . . .

Dennis   Why yu love to put me down?

Gravel   . . . me done!

Dennis   If I go Mama, I go live in London. Dass ware Granger was born? Tell me about London, Pops.

Gravel   It a dirty nasty place.

Hope   London is very nice.

Gravel   How would yu know?

Hope   It aways look nice when deh show it in a flim.

Gravel   Wat is my wife talking about?

Hope   Las' one I see, dis couple walk by de river – wat it called? Thames – de moon was out, it was night, it look so romantic.

Gravel (*mimicking*)   Oh it were so romantic! Who was in de movie, let me guess, Stewart-blasted-Granger? Batayman.

Dennis   Wat?

Hope   Stewart Granger no batayman!

Gravel   Im a batayman.

Hope   Im have a whole heap a woman.

Gravel   Men too. 'Im and Cary Grant having a lickle ting.

Dennis (*shocked*)   Cary Grant!

Hope   Juss ignore 'im Dennis.

Dennis   Cary Grant!

Hope   Dennis!

Dennis   I don't know now Mama, I not so sure now.

Hope   Das not yu said a minute ago.

Dennis   But why be all friendly to a bwoy 'im hardly know?

Hope   Ca' 'im a nice man, like yu say. Don't be so stupid.

Dennis   I not stupid! Pops, yer wrong.

Gravel   Awright. But when yu drop yer hat, kick it home.

Dennis (*he gets it*)   Hey!

Hope   Bwoy shut up. (*To* **Gravel**.) Is ware yu hear all dis?

Gravel Yu be surprised wat Gravel hear on de streets a London. It a sinful place, Gravel keep telling yu. Yu wanna know wat it like Dennis? One time me an' yer Uncle Neville get a job working in sum bar in London. It seem awright, till we see two men coming in holding hands, kissing! Gravel ask Neville, wat kinda club is dis?

Hope Places like dat exist all over Gravel.

Gravel Not here deh don't.

Hope Oh no? Yer wan' tek look down Harbor Street, de two a yu.

Dennis Na das awright.

Gravel Gravel not finished.

Hope So finish.

Gravel Next ting we know, police come kicking down de door, everyone run like rat, who get catch?

Dennis Yu an' Uncle Neville?

Gravel Im gone, run off. He aways did dat. Leaving me to clear up 'im mess.

Dennis It'll never happen to me man.

Gravel Oh yu tink so?

Dennis I not like yu Pops, when trouble come, me run.

Gravel Yu don' tink I tried?

Dennis Not hard enough.

Gravel Deh arrested me.

Dennis But not Uncle Neville, ca' 'im smart. Shoulda tumped dem in de head and run. It wat me woulda done.

Gravel How?

Dennis Wat?

Gravel How? Show me how bwoy.

Hope   Gravel?

Gravel   Gravel wat! I wan' me son to show me. Show me bwoy. Yu afraid?

Dennis *holds up his fists.*

Gravel   Now, come an' hit me. Wat yu laughin' fer?

Dennis   I don't wan' hit yu Pops.

Gravel   Prove I raise no weak bwoy.

Hope   Tek it easy please.

Gravel (*brushing her away*)   Don't do yer daddy no favours now, right?

Hope   Stop dis.

Gravel   Come on!

Dennis *does not want to do this. He clips* **Gravel** *on the cheek.*

Gravel   Gravel say hit not tickle.

Dennis *goes to hit him but* **Gravel** *dodges around him a few times.*

Gravel   Yu not hitting me bwoy.

Hope   Slow down.

Gravel   Yer daddy too quick fer yu?

Dennis   No.

Gravel   Yu lie!

Dennis   I don't wan' to hit yu pops.

Gravel (*shoving him hard*)   Yu tink yu better than me right? Is dat wat yu tink!

Hope   Come on . . .

Gravel   Is dat wat yu tink Dennis?

Dennis   It wat I know.

Gravel *throws a punch of his own, striking* **Dennis** *in the face.*

Hope   Gravel!

Gravel   See it deh! Like lightning.

Hope   Let me see . . .

Dennis   I'm fine! (*Leaves the yard.*)

Hope   Why?

Gravel   Im not goin' to Englan', Hope.

Hope   Das up to 'im man.

Gravel   Im not goin' all dat way to follow 'im daddy right. 'Im not followin' Neville.

Hope   Gravel, yu is 'im fudda.

Gravel   He got too much a 'im daddy in 'im.

Hope   Don' say dat.

Gravel   He even had to grow up wid de same face.

Hope   So wat man? It don' matter. It doesn't matter Gravel. It yu who raise 'im. Yu is 'im fudda. Yu can't keep blamin' Neville fer all dis.

Gravel   Gravel blaming yu. From de day de bwoy could talk, yer tekin' 'im to see flim.

Hope   And so?

Gravel   So how many times I watch yu riding off on de back a Neville's bike to see flim? How many times?

Hope   Yu nuh see de man in twenty years, and yer still jealous a 'im.

Gravel   Ca' yu mek me see 'im!

Hope   How? How am I doing dat?

Gravel   Sonny Blake.

Hope   God's sake nuh man.

Gravel   Joe Newman.

Hope   Ancient history, Gravel.

Gravel   Walford! 'Bout ancient history.

Hope   Gravel . . .

Gravel   Yer own nephew, my sister's child. Yu is dirty nasty woman. Don't tell me I nuh see my broder in twenty years right, nuh tell me dat. Ca' yu still wan' 'im.

Hope   I married yu. I love yu.

Gravel   But yu still wan' 'im. Yu wan' 'im Hope. Tell me say yu wan' im, tell me say yu wan' im, tell me yu say yu want him Hope . . .

Hope   Gravel . . .

Gravel   Tell me say yu wan' 'im.

Hope   Stop it.

Gravel   Tell me.

Hope   Awright I wan' 'im! I wan' 'im to mek love to me like he used to on de beach, I wan' to feel 'im hands strokin' my thigh, I wanna feel my hands touchin' 'im chest, 'im face, I wan' feel love dat mek me live a whole lifetime's-worth in one night! Yu happy now, is dat wat yu wan' fer me to say to yu?

Gravel   Awright den, Gravel tired right. First ting tomorrow, I go draw out my money from de bank and give yu.

Hope   Wat yu chat 'bout now?

Gravel   Yu go Englan'. No more talk or dreamin' right? Yu go find 'im.

Hope   I go Englan', and who go tek care a yu?

Gravel   I DON'T NEED NOBODY TO TEK CARE A ME!

Gravel *holds his chest.*

Hope   Gravel? Oh my Lord no Gravel, come, come Gravel, come. Don't fight me, come on.

Hope *takes* **Gravel** *inside.*

In the street. **Pammy** *is nursing* **Dennis**'s *bleeding face.*

Dennis   I shoulda knock 'im head right off!

Pammy   Yu can't do dat.

Dennis   He nearly do it to me.

Pammy   Wat yu do to mek 'im angry?

Dennis   Yeah gw'n, tek 'im side like yer aways do. Dis is de way 'im is Pammy, I keep telling but yer nuh believe me. He can't stand de fact that I better than 'im. And I am. No one laugh at me. Yu hear anyone call me Midas? Yu know how many times I had to fight oder bwoys at school who were calling 'im names? An' were 'im grateful? (*Mimics.*) 'Gravel don't need yu fighting my battles!' Now it Lickle Hope's turn to fight, I feel sorry fer her. I ain't letting my pikne go through dat. Gonna give dem wat de wan', deh dreams go come true. Can I stay wid yu tonight?

Pammy   Dennis.

Dennis   I won't mek noise. Come on Pammy, please.

Pammy   Yu can sleep on de floor.

Dennis   Floor bad fer my back. Can't I share de bed wid yu? I nuh snore. (**Pammy** *hits him.*) Pammy!

Pammy   Move from me before I mek yer whole body bleed.

Dennis   All me say man . . .

Pammy   I know wat yu said. Got it all planned right? Come over here fer a lickle sympathy den get me into bed.

Dennis   No Pammy.

Pammy   Yes Dennis!

Dennis   Look I had a bad day yer nuh . . .

Pammy   And I haven't? It aways about yu Dennis. Yu an' yer pops fighting again, yu and yer stupid flim, running from Lester. Yu ever stop to tink about me? Yu ever ask 'How was yer day Pammy?'

Dennis   How was yer day Pammy?

Pammy   Awful.

Dennis   Why wat happen?

Pammy   Wass de point, yu don't care. Yu juss wan' tek me to bed so yer can tell Wally an' all yer friends.

Dennis   Wat happen?

Pammy   Mama had to throw sum man out ca' 'im getting too rough wid her. He wan'ed her to do all kind a nasty tings. Next ting I know 'im following me to de shop, he grabbed me from behind, sayin' in my ear if my mama won't do it, he go mek me do it. I kick 'im so hard and run.

Dennis   De nasty sunafabitch! Who was it? Tell me who it was, Pammy, I break 'im neck.

Pammy   I don't wan' yu breakin' anyone's neck.

Dennis   Pammy, no one does dat to yu an' lives right? Yu hearing me?

Pammy   I wan' yu to understand, understand me.

Dennis   I do understand yu.

Pammy   De only reason that man come after me Dennis ca' he tinks I juss like me mudda. Everyone tinks I like me mudda. I can't give yu wat yer wan' – not till I sure.

Dennis   Feel my heart, Pammy. Feel it.

Pammy (*with her hand on his chest*)   It like a drum gone mad.

Dennis   It goes like dat, every time I wid yu. Everytime I see yu. Yu everyting to me, yer de only ting on dis island worth staying fer, Pammy Simpson.

Pammy   Am I?

Dennis   Wat more me have to do to prove it? (*Kisses her, unbuttons her blouse.*)

Pammy   Don't ever hurt me Dennis.

Scene Two

Weeks later. **Hope** *is in her usual spot, on top of the car, watching the film with the binoculars.*

Hope   Gw'n Granger, teach dem sum manners.

Wally *enters the yard, he squeezes her behind.*

Hope   Walford!

Wally   Sorry Auntie.

Hope   Wat yu wan'?

Wally   Suck on yer tittie till me eye pop out. Dem still filmin'?

Hope   Shush.

Wally   Dem can't hear.

Wally *tries to distract* **Hope**'s *attention by running his hand up and down her leg.*

Hope   Stop it.

Wally   No one here.

Hope   I don't care. I wan' watch dis awright?

Wally   Come on.

Hope   Yu got three minutes.

Wally   Wat?

Hope   Dem reloading de camera, it aways tek dem 'bout three minutes.

Wally   Wat yu expect me to do in three minutes?

Hope   Tell me wat yu wan'.

Wally   Guess!

Hope (*slaps his hand away*)   No!

Wally   Dis woman drive me mad!

Hope   Yu nuh even ask how yer uncle doing.

Wally (*uninterested*)   How Uncle Gravel doing?

Hope   He coulda dead yu nuh Walford?

Wally   Awright, so how 'im doing?

Hope   Im fine, 'im tekin' it easy now.

Wally   Good, now come home wid me.

Hope   I watchin' de flim.

Wally   But me ting get big. Yu wan' me to show yu? Hope? Wat me do?

Hope   Who yu bin talkin' to Wally?

Wally   Nobody.

Hope   So how come Pammy and Gravel know?

Wally   Deh know?

Hope   How come deh know? Yu shooting off yer mout, tellin' how yer bin grinding a married woman? Is that how deh hear? So how come deh know den?

Wally   Deh musta guess.

Hope   Wat yu bin sayin' to mek dem guess?

Wally   Nuttin! Look, look I don't even care, right? Pammy won't say anyting, Gravel nuttin but a jackass and 'im sick, wat can he do?

Hope   Don't yu dare talk about my husband so.

Wally   We be more careful.

Hope   No Walford. No more.

Wally   Yu mad.

Hope   It not up to yu.

Wally   I is no door yu can juss open and shut yu nuh.

Hope   Yu tink I go let yu mek fool a me?

Wally   Me sorry.

Hope   Don' beg.

Wally   Me nuh beg.

Hope   Yer three minutes up.

Wally   Is wat yer wan' from me den? Yer wan' fer me to carry sword, kill whole heap a men, jump through window like Stewart Granger? Mek women dead fer me? Is dat de kinda man yer wan'?

Hope   At least he can never hurt me.

Wally   I wan' love yu.

Hope   Yu wan' fuck me!

Wally   Me love yu.

Hope   Wally yu is juss a bwoy. Gw'n awright, lemme.

Wally   Yu wan' half a Kingston to know 'bout us, oder half laughin' at Uncle Gravel?

Hope   An' de rest to watch yer mama throw yer arse out, right before yer fudda knock off yer stupid lickle head! And yu know he will. Yu lickle fool.

Wally   Too bad Dennis got a mama like yu, all it tek fer sumone to open 'im mouth, an' boom, he know de trut. He might wan' to do summin stupid, come after me. Last ting I wan', fer me to hurt me cousin Auntie.

Hope   Stay away from my son. 'Im worth ten a yu.

Wally   Im a bwoy too.

Hope   Im special.

Wally   So special he mek Pammy pregnant?

Hope   Wat?

Wally   Her mudda tell me de oder day. I sorry. Look at me. Juss tell me wat yu wan' Hope . . .

Hope   Get out, get out.

Wally   Yu don't wan' my ting? Nuff gyals wan' my ting!

Wally *leaves.* **Hope** *goes back into the house.*

Little Hope *and* **Dennis** *come running into the yard shortly afterwards, shooting at each other with their fingers as guns. They play around all over the yard until* **Dennis** *clutches his heart and drops down dead.* **Little Hope** *continues to shoot at him while he's down. She eventually stops.*

Little Hope   Dennis?

Dennis   Yeah?

Little Hope   Yu dead?

Dennis   Mash up.

They both laugh as they tickle each other.

Gravel (*coming out*)   Yu plannin' on lying on de ground all day?

Little Hope   Daddy!

Little Hope *runs over to give her father a hug.*

Gravel   Easy chile yer wan' give me more pain?

Little Hope   Yu supposed to be resting in bed.

Gravel   Oh yu my nurse now?

Little Hope   Yes!

Gravel   No, yu is me pride!

Little Hope   We got a surprise fer yu Daddy, show 'im Dennis, show 'im.

Dennis *turns on the engine. It is running smoothly.*

Gravel   Wat de hell?

Little Hope   Dennis bin working on it all week Daddy.

Gravel   How?

Dennis   Few hours, mostly at night.

Gravel   No. (*Points to the car.*) How?

Dennis   Engine older than yu Pops, but she like me.

Little Hope   I helped as well Daddy. I tink yu should call de business Gravel & Son & Daughter. Wait!

Little Hope *heads for the house.*

Gravel   Ware yu goin'?

Gravel *and* **Dennis** *remain silent, neither sure what to say to the other.* **Little Hope** *returns with a camera.*

Little Hope   Put yer arm round 'im Daddy, come on.

Gravel *and* **Dennis** *pose nervously as* **Little Hope** *takes their picture. She runs to the fence and starts climbing.*

Gravel   Chile why yu nuh use de door? Ware yu going?

Little Hope   Tell me friends no one laughs at my pops no more. (*Exit.*)

Gravel   Yu ever see dat chile keep still?

Dennis   Nope. Yu had me scared yu nuh Pops.

Gravel   Is dat why yu do it, ca' yu wan' favour?

Dennis   No.

Gravel   Nuttin changed right.

Dennis   Right.

Gravel   Yu still too rude.

Dennis   Yep.

Gravel *turns the engine on again. He loves the sound of what he is hearing but tries not to show it.*

Gravel   Why yu watch me fer? Shouldn't yu be off actin'?

Dennis   Later. I bin counting all de things deh got me doing, I going to be in five different scenes yer nuh Pops, five.

Gravel *takes out his flask.* **Dennis** *takes the flask off him.*

Gravel   Gimme back me flask!

Dennis   Yu know ware dis drink going?

Gravel   Down my throat, gimme!

Dennis *pours the drink on to the ground.*

Gravel   Yu see de problem wid yu is right, yu never had enough licks as a child.

Dennis   Ca' me too fast fer yu.

Gravel   Ca' yu aways hide behind yer mudda. 'Mummy, Mummy, Daddy wan' hit me!' She never use belt on yer tail once.

Dennis   Yeah, give de child sum licks.

Gravel   Wat else is deh?

Dennis   Talkin'? Find out why de child do wat 'im do.

Gravel   Child do wat 'im do ca' 'im too renk. Nuttin wrong wid licks, when fuddas tell deh pikne to do summin, deh do it, or deh get licks. Don' mean yu don' love dem.

Dennis   Yu nuh feel de child need to hear it?

Gravel   Is which flim yu hear dat? I keep tellin' yu dem Hollywood people don't know nuttin 'bout life.

Dennis   Well yu'll be pleased to know deh nearly finish.

Gravel   Good.

Dennis   Deh all be going home.

Gravel   Good.

Dennis   I go to Englan' Pops.

Gravel   When?

Dennis   Soon. I got my money save. I showed Granger my speech from *Romeo an' Juliet*, he say I should audition for dat school RADA. I go soon.

Gravel   Yu juss go jump on a boat, show yer speech to dem people an' boom! Deh let yu in? (*Laughs.*)

Dennis   Why is dat so hard fer yu?

Gravel   Yu don't know nuttin 'bout wat out deh Dennis.

Dennis   Tell me den.

Gravel   Yu only wan' wat yu wan' to hear.

Dennis   I wanna hear yu.

Gravel   Awright. Gravel leave 'im home ca' he wan' see de rest a de world.

Dennis   Yeah?

Gravel   Gravel see de world fer wat it is, nasty dirty place . . .

Dennis   Pops?

Gravel   . . . so he come back to 'im home, ware 'im belong.

Dennis   Das not . . .

Gravel   . . . not wat yu wan' to hear? Yu see wat I mean?

Dennis   Wat about Uncle Neville den?

Gravel   Wat dis have to do wid im?

Dennis   Im still deh.

Gravel   Wid 'im white woman, wid my money 'im tief!

Dennis   Don't mean it go happen to me. I not like yu. I could be de first Jamaican ever to win Oscar. De first!

Gravel   Das yer mudda talkin' bwoy. I suppose she tell yu to go.

Dennis   She tell me I should do wass right fer me.

Gravel   And wat about Pammy? Yer fiancée, in case yu ferget.

Dennis   She'll find sumone else. Sumone better right?

Gravel   Yu could do a whole lot worse than her yu know son. She a lovely gyal Dennis.

Dennis   I know dat. But I have to do dis. Don't go on awright.

Gravel   Juss tell me summin right . . .

Dennis   No!

Gravel   All dem flims yer mama tek yu to see, yu ever see one wid a black man in de lead?

Dennis   No.

Gravel   See dat James Bond flim Dr watimname . . .

Dennis   *Dr No.*

Gravel   Right. James Bond 'im have a friend?

Dennis   Quarrel?

Gravel   Quarrel! Now 'im smart right, good wid a knife, drive a boat, everyting. So how come it 'im who have de carry de man shoes, who get kill by dat dragon ting?

Dennis   Ca' 'im save Bond life.

Gravel   Why?

Dennis   Ca' Bond de hero.

Gravel   Why?

Dennis   Ca' 'im James Bond, Pops!

Gravel   Why? Why couldn't Bond be de one dat get dead up and . . .

Dennis   Yu can't kill James Bond.

Gravel   . . . Quarrel have de gyal? Gravel know why. It wat white people wan' it, it way it go stay. Deh don' wan' us deh.

Dennis   But I can change tings Pops, I wan' to try, is why yu never listen . . .

Gravel   De Alamo, Johnny Wayne! Juss before de Mexicans come and kill up everybody, Johnny Wayne let 'im slave go, tell 'im he a free man. So wat de fool go an' do, decide to stay so he can get kill up wid everyone else. If dat were me right, Gravel would be sayin' to Johnny Wayne 'Me gone. It my black arse me a look out fer'.

Dennis   Richard Widmark.

Gravel   Wat yu say?

Dennis   Richard Widmark had de slave Pops, not Johnny Wayne.

Gravel   It don't matter. Cha, Gravel finish wid yu.

Dennis   Gravel finish wid yu, Gravel tell yu why, Gravel go mek us all rich. Why should Dennis listen to yu?

Gravel Yu wan' go, go.

Dennis I will.

Gravel Gravel say no more to yu. (*Goes inside.*)

Dennis Good. I going to England! (**Hope** *comes outside.*)
Hey Mama, Mama? Who star wid Errol Flynn in *Robin Hood*
in 1939 . . . ?

Hope *slaps his face.*

Dennis Sorry.

Hope Wat yu sorry fer?

Dennis Fer wat I done. Yu wan' tell me wat it is?

Hope Yu see Pammy lately?

Dennis Mama don't start.

Hope Dat mean no.

Dennis I juss had Pops man, I'll tell her.

Hope Yu know wat she telling people? She pregnant, yu
is de fudda!

Dennis Wat?

Hope Bwoy have I not tell a thousand times, to use
summin?

Dennis I didn't think.

Hope I know yu didn't think!

Dennis It all happen quick, I didn't have time . . .

Hope Don' tell me I don' wan' to know.

Dennis I gotta see her man.

Hope Yu mad? She blaming yu, when it could be a whole
line a men.

Dennis Pammy not like dat.

Hope   Oh come on.

Dennis   She's not.

Hope   So wat yu sayin'?

Dennis   De baby mine. I know it.

Hope   It money she after.

Dennis   Oh Mama!

Hope   Fine don' listen to me, throw away yer life.

Dennis   I tell yu Pammy not like . . .

Hope   . . . like that! An' I tellin' yu from de moment me lay eyes pon de gyal I see trouble. Yu got all yer money saved Dennis, wat yu tink go happen if de child is yours? Leave it, let sum oder fool tek care a her, yu got dreams, plans, yu wan' throw it all away?

Dennis   No but. . . .

Hope   Deh is no but Dennis. I nuh raise yu to be like everyone else right. Ca' I tellin' yu years from now, when I sittin' in de theatre and I see yer name, yer face up on de big screen, I wan' to jump up and shout at all dem fools, and say das my bwoy! 'Im done it! 'Im special. Yu special Dennis?

Dennis   Yeah bu . . .

Hope   Dennis! Yu special?

Dennis   Yes Mama.

Hope   Right. Not a word to yer fudda.

Scene Three

Back yard. Night time. **Pammy** *is alone, drunk, and screaming her head off.*

Pammy   Dennis! I wan' to talk to yu. Don't ignore me bwoy! Dennis! Dennis! Denni . . .

Hope *comes out of the house.*

Pammy   I wan' to see Dennis.

Hope   Hush up Pamela, yu know wat time it is? 'Im not here.

Pammy   Dennis!

Hope   Gyal yu drunk?

Pammy   Wat yu care?

Hope   Yu supposed to be pregnant, yu don't know drink could harm de baby?

Pammy   Dennis . . .

Hope   Sweetheart I know wat yu goin' through.

Pammy   Move! 'Bout yu pretendin' yu nice. Yu couldn't wait to tell 'im.

Hope   Why didn't yu?

Pammy   Dis is between me an' Dennis.

Hope   Yu really tink my son go marry yu, whore like yer moder.

Pammy *makes a run at her.* **Hope** *holds her down.*

Hope   Yu wan' fight me Pamela? How much money yu wan'? How much yu wan' to get rid a it? Wat yu tink go happen here? Dennis give up 'im whole life juss to be wid yu? Men like Dennis are birds Pammy, deh have to spread dem wings and fly, not get lock up in a cage, wat we have to hold dem back. Wat we have to offer dem? Wat yu have dat de rest a us don' have Pammy? Yu got nuttin right. How much?

Gravel (*coming out*)   Hope! Stop it. Stop it! It awright Pammy, it awright. How long yu know?

Pammy   A few weeks.

Gravel   So why yu nuh say nuttin before?

Pammy   He'll tink I did it on purpose.

Gravel   It tek two to mek baby Pammy.

Pammy   Wally open 'im big mouth.

Gravel   Wally know as well? Look yu don' worry 'bout a ting right Pammy, we go wait right here fer Dennis and sort dis out.

Hope   No. Yu wan' ruin our son's life?

Gravel   I don' wan' hear anudda word from yu.

Hope   Yu talk to me like dat in front a her?

Gravel   Look at her Hope, look at her. Dis is yu yu nuh.

Hope   Don' tell her our business.

Gravel   Yu wan' her to go through wat yu did? Yu wan' her to sit at home wid baby, marry man she don't love perhaps, while she wait every night, pray fer Dennis to come tek her away? No Hope! Dis time no one get away.

Pammy   Hold on a second, yu not Dennis' fudda. (*Laughs.*)

Hope   I wan' break yer neck.

Pammy   Wa' wrong Hope, yu couldn' keep holda yer own man, he don' wan' yu? Serve yu right.

Gravel   Das enuff Pamela.

Pammy   Wat?

Gravel   Yu don' talk back to me wife like dat.

Pammy   Why yu so stupid? She mek fool a yu again yu, she doin' it now.

Hope   Throw de bitch out.

Pammy   Ask her 'bout her and Wally . . .

Hope   Throw her out Gravel.

Pammy   Ask her nuh man.

Gravel   Gravel know!

Pammy   An' yu nuh lick her in de head? I never wan' believe wat people say about yu.

Gravel   But yu did right? Come like de rest a dem, laugh at Gravel.

Pammy   I never laugh.

Gravel   Go home Pammy.

Pammy   Not once.

Gravel   Don' worry 'bout a ting right, Gravel sort dis out. Go home!

Gravel *hurries* **Pammy** *out.*

Hope   Yu don't know de baby his. Yu said yu let 'im go.

Gravel *switches on the car engine.*

Gravel   Hear dat? My son do dis. My son!

Hope   Yu really tink 'im go stay?

Gravel   Im have a heart Hope.

Hope   Are yu so stupid?

Gravel   Someware. Ware yu and Neville nuh have 'im. 'Im have a heart . . .

Hope *slaps his face.*

Gravel   See wat Neville do to yu.

Hope   Dis isn't about Neville. Jesus yu island men are all de same wid yer small minds and nuttin else, yu knew how me felt when we got married. Look 'pon yerself Gravel. Look 'pon yerself, yu really wan' Dennis to be like yu?

Gravel   Yu tink yer so special, but yer nuttin.

Hope   Bwoy like Neville, like 'im real fudda and yu can't stand dat!

Hope *turns round to see* **Dennis** *who arrived a moment earlier. He turns round and leaves the way he came.*

Hope   Dennis.

Scene Four

Back yard two days later. **Dennis** *enters, being pushed into the yard by* **Lester**.

Lester   I only bringing yer here ca' yer fudda is a friend, but if yu joke wid me again right, once more, I go bus' yer head an' throw yer arse in jail.

Dennis   So do it den. Tek me to jail. Yu fat rass . . .

Lester   Shut yer mout.

Dennis   It bottle a rum yu wan'. Yu juss like dem, liar.

Lester (*swings his baton*)   I'll do it yer nuh.

Gravel *comes out of the house.*

Lester   Gravel! Yu never guess ware me find 'im. On top a Wally Mitchell, deh were both beatin' each oder nearly half to death, Lord knows why. Deh mek aright mess a Joey's bar. I had to arrest 'im.

Gravel   Tek 'im den. (**Lester** *laughs.*) Yu hear me tell joke?

Lester   No. But I tought . . .

Gravel   Wat?

Lester *eyes* **Dennis** *laughing to himself.*

Lester   I hear yu get de car running? Lot a people tought yu couldn't do it. But not me. Gravel Gilbey got 'im fudda's hands. Dat was a nice bottle a rum yer give my fudda Gravel. 'Im bin talkin' 'bout it fer days.

Gravel   Deh's none left.

Lester   Well das a shame. I go have to tek 'im in Gravel.

Gravel   So tek 'im.

Lester   Awright. (*To* **Dennis**.) Come.

Gravel   I'll come wid yu.

Lester (*suspicious*)   Good.

Gravel   I tell yer captain how much yu an' yer fudda enjoyed my rum!

Lester   Juss yu keep an eye on 'im right. Ca' next time I bus' 'im head!

Gravel   So long Lester.

Lester *exits.*

Dennis   Yu wan' fer me to say tanks?

Gravel   Yer tink I wan' anyting from yu?

Dennis   Fine den.

Gravel   Good!

Dennis   Right!

Gravel *gets in the car.*

I hope yer crash.

Gravel   Wat?

Dennis   Nuttin.

Gravel   Yu 'fraid to speak up?

Dennis (*throws something*)   Present fer yu. Wally's front teet'. Ca' yu not man enough to do it yerself. Yu not even sorry.

Gravel   Sorry fer wat? Wat Gravel got to be sorry fer?

Dennis   If yu weren't sick man.

Gravel   Yer punch me out? Gravel de one who should be doing de punching round here. Yu see Pammy?

Dennis   Don' change de subject.

Gravel   Have yu?

Dennis   No.

Gravel   I see.

Dennis   Yeah Pops yu see, I Neville Gilbey's bwoy right, das wat yu see. Me juss like 'im. Yu call yerself a man?

Gravel   Man? Yu is a man Dennis?

Dennis   More than yu!

Gravel   Yes so all dis time I see yu, actin' all nice and sweet wid dat gyal, waitin' to get wat yu wan'. An' when yu finally get it, when she need yu de most, yu throw her away like sum rubbish, oh yes Dennis, yu are a man.

Dennis   It weren't like dat.

Gravel   Yu don' love de gyal.

Dennis   I do.

Gravel   So badly yu wan' leave her?

Dennis   Wat am I supposed to do den, yu tell me.

Gravel   Yu do wass right.

Dennis   Pops I can't.

Gravel   Den yu is nuttin.

Dennis   Stop lookin' at me like I 'im right. I don't even know de man.

Gravel   Yu his son.

Dennis   Yu my fudda. Wat I am is ca' a yu.

Gravel   Wat yu are is ca' a im, ca' a yer mudda . . .

Dennis   And yu!

Gravel *starts the car up.*

Dennis   Yeah gw'n den!

A loud bang from the engine. Smoke rises from the bonnet. **Dennis** *shouts his father's name as he runs over to him. He pulls him out of the car.*

Gravel   Yu tell me yu fix it! (**Dennis** *laughs.*) Shut up.

Dennis   I mus be yer son Pops.

Gravel   Useless!

Dennis   Like yu.

Gravel (*shakes his head*)   Neville's bwoy.

Dennis   I yer bwoy.

Gravel   Neville's bwoy!

Dennis   I wan' act Pops, I wan' life! Ain't dat why yu went England, to get life? I awready tell people I going man. If I stay, deh go laugh at me too, hear dem now, Gravel wife and 'im nephew Wally . . .

Gravel   Shut yer mout!

Dennis   I don' wan' dat.

Gravel   It wat yu feel inside dat matters.

Dennis   Why yu have to come back? Yu can't you see wat it done to yu? Well I not go die here like yu. Mama could be right yer nuh, how yu know it my baby? Pammy a Simpson, she juss like she mudda.

Gravel   Yu really believe dat?

Dennis   Yes!

Gravel   Den on yer way Neville's bwoy. Gravel try and give yu an' yer mudda a decent life and look wat yer do wid it. Gravel come back ca' a de two a yu. Yu know how long I was in Englan' before Neville decide to tell me she was pregnant? A year! An' like a fool me come back, ca' like a fool me marry her, ca' like a stupid fool Gravel love her all 'im life. (*Takes a deep breath.*)

Dennis   Pops?

Gravel   Dennis gw'n inside and get me my medicine.

Dennis   Wat?

Gravel   I'll fetch it myself. (*Clutches his heart.*)

Dennis   Pops!

Dennis *runs inside the house. He comes back out with* **Gravel**'*s tablets.*

Dennis   Come on Pops, yer not sick, yu juss worked up a lickle right? Pops? I go fetch de doctor. (**Gravel** *holds his son's hand.*) Lemme go Pops, lemme go man.

Dennis *runs out.*

Gravel (*in pain*)   God! (*Feels the last beat in his heart.*) Hope?

Scene Five

Back yard. One week later. **Little Hope** *is alone on stage polishing the car.* **Dennis** *comes out to help her.* **Little Hope** *grabs his rag and throws it to the ground.* **Dennis** *picks it up,* **Little Hope** *grabs it from him again and does the same thing.*

Dennis   I only tryin' to help Lickle Hope.

Little Hope (*snaps*)   Hope! Stop calling me Lickle Hope.

Dennis   Sorry. (*Picks up his rag.*)

Little Hope   I cleaning Daddy's car! Leave it. Yu aways mek 'im upset. Yu kill 'im. I hate yu.

Dennis   Yu go get yer dress all dirty.

Little Hope   Daddy aways let me wear pants.

Little Hope *walks to the house, she passes* **Pammy** *who gently taps her on the head.*

Little Hope   I look like doll to yu?

Pammy   No.

Little Hope   Yu stupid?

Dennis   Hey, Lickle Hope.

Little Hope   My name is Hope!

Dennis (*snaps*)   Get inside.

Pammy *watches* **Dennis** *polishing the car.*

Dennis   Tought I might tek it out yu nuh, see how it go.

Pammy   Good.

Dennis   Wan' come?

Pammy   Awright.

Dennis   Little Hope said I kill im, she right yer nuh?

Pammy   Don't say dat.

Dennis   I keep seein' 'im face Pammy.

Pammy   Don't.

Dennis   Pay no attention right, Dennis juss upset.

Dennis *sees* **Hope** *standing by the door, watching. This prompts him to kiss* **Pammy** *on the lips.*

Pammy   Dennis . . .

Dennis *kisses her again.*

Leave de car fer a minute.

Hope   Yu wan' summin from de store Dennis?

Dennis   Car look good yu tink?

Pammy   Yes.

Hope   Do yu wan' summin from de store Dennis?

Dennis   Watch me now Pops.

Hope   Sooner or later yu go have to speak to me.

Pammy   Come Dennis let's go fer a ride now.

Hope   Look at me.

Pammy   Juss leave 'im.

Hope   Dennis?

Dennis   I not sellin' de car Mama.

Hope   Yu hear me say yu should?

Dennis   Yu can't wait to get rid a everyting that was Pops can yu?

Hope   I loved yer fudda.

Dennis   Hear dat Pammy, she loved Pops.

Hope   I haven't got de strength to fight yu awright.

Dennis   Juss get me a bokkle a pop from de shop and leave me alone right.

Hope   I soon come.

Dennis   So wat about me bin so special den? Dat lie too?

Hope   Wat yu wan' fer me to say?

Dennis   I not Neville's bwoy, I can't be, I Gravel's bwoy right?

Hope   Yer no one's bwoy Dennis, yu belong to yerself.

Dennis   Whose am I Mama? Juss tell me dat, or yu don't know.

Hope *walks out of the yard without saying anything.*

Pammy   I hate her. I know she yer mama but I really hate her . . .

Dennis   Awright Pammy, wa wrong wid yu? Yu have me.

Pammy   Have I?

Dennis (*snaps*)   Yes!

Pammy   How yu feel Dennis?

Dennis   Fine, juss fine. Wat, yu don' believe me?

Pammy   I wan' to.

Dennis   'But soft, what light through yonder window breaks? It is the East, and Juliet is the sun!'

Pammy   Come inside. Dennis?

Dennis *finds a piece of wood and paints something on it.*

Pammy   Dennis? Dennis!

Dennis *can hear but ignores her.* **Pammy** *leaves the yard. Dennis finishes painting. The sign now reads,* Gravel & Son. **Dennis** *places it against the car window. He stares at it.* **Dennis** *drops his head.*

End.

Lift Off

Lift Off was first performed at the Royal Court Theatre Upstairs, London, on 19 February 1999. The cast was as follows:

Hannah	Sarah Cakebread
Young Mal	Ashley Chin
Rich	Mohammed George
Young Tone	Sid Mitchell
Mal	Michael Price
Carol	Laura Sadler
Tone	Alex Walkinshaw

Directed by Indhu Rubasingham
Designed by Ultz
Lighting by Ultz and Marion Mahon
Music by Paul Arditti

Part One

A kids' playground in the middle of a council estate, somewhere in west London.

Rich, *a young black schoolboy, enters and climbs up on the monkey bars. He reaches the top and makes himself comfortable. He opens his sports bag and takes out one of his schoolbooks. He rips out a page and begins folding, continuing to fold and bend the paper until it resembles an aeroplane.* **Rich** *looks very pleased with his creation. He holds out his other arm and aims along it.*

He is disturbed by the sound of two boys arguing. **Young Mal** *and* **Young Tone** *enter.*

Young Tone   And yer mum Mal!

Young Mal   I bloody did right.

Young Tone   Yu love to chat outta yer arse.

Young Mal   It happened Tony.

Young Tone   Tone. My name is Tone now. Cha rahtid man.

Young Mal (*sarcastic*)   Sorry, Tone!

Rich   Wat appened?

Young Tone/Young Mal   Chinny!

The boys run over to **Rich**. *They each take turns squeezing and holding on to his chin.* **Rich** *just waits for them to finish.*

Young Mal   My turn, my turn.

Young Tone   Move!

Young Mal   Ooh! That was good.

Young Tone   Ennit!

Rich   So wat appened?

Young Tone   This turd . . .

Young Mal   Don't call me a turd, yer mum's a turd.

Young Tone   He reckons right, he ran all the way to the school gates from here in five minutes.

Young Mal   Yeah!

Young Tone   Even dough right, it takes twenty minutes to get there by bus.

Young Mal   Yeah!

Young Tone   And yer mum!

Young Mal   I timed it myself.

Young Tone   Yu aint even got a watch yu tramp.

Young Mal   I counted it in my head.

Rich   If yer gonna tell a lie Mal, make it a good one.

Young Tone   Thank yu Rich.

Young Mal   I aint lyin.

Young Tone   Yu aint tellin the trut.

Young Mal   Wat yu know?

Young Tone   Suck my dick.

Young Mal   Queer.

Young Tone   I aint a queer, yer a queer, yer de biggest batayman on de estate!

Young Mal   And yer a paedophile.

Young Tone   And yer a necrophilia.

Young Mal   Wat yu call me?

Young Tone   Tell him Rich.

Rich   Yu like shaggin dead people.

Young Mal   Yu wanna slap?

Young Tone   Bruno!

Young Mal   I'll kick yer arse.

Young Tone   Come now if yer bad.

Young Mal   No yu come here.

Young Tone   No yu come here.

Young Mal   Yu come here.

Young Tone   Yu come here first.

Young Mal   No.

Young Tone   Yer soft man. Blood clart.

Young Mal   Cha rahtid.

Young Tone   Cha rass clart.

Young Mal   Blouse and skirt nuh man.

Young Tone   Shut yer boomba hole bwai!

Young Mal   Yer batayman wid yer donkey face.

Young Tone   Oh fuck me irie man.

Young Mal *laughs.*

Young Tone   Wat?

Young Mal   Yu can't fuck an irie, yu fish.

Young Tone   Yu can.

Young Mal   Yu can't. Irie means yer cool, yer safe, everyting awright. (*Laughs.*) Fuck me irie.

Young Tone   Awright then I'll fuck yer mum.

Young Mal   Yu wanna slap?

Young Tone   Yu wanna try?

Young Mal   Yer mum sucks dicks for a livin'.

Rich   Ware's mine?

Young Tone   Ware's wat?

Rich   My ice cream?

Young Tone   Oh sorry Rich, fergot ennit.

Rich   Yu didn't ferget yours.

Young Tone   Yeah, so?

Rich   It was my money.

Young Tone   Yeah, so?

Rich   Don't laugh at me.

Young Mal   Don't be so wet Rich.

Rich   I really fancied an ice cream.

Young Tone   Errgh! He fancies an ice cream.

Rich   No.

Young Mal   It's wat yu said.

Young Mal   Yu wanna wank over it and eat it up Rich.

Rich   Yer nasty.

Young Tone   And yu've got skid marks like Danny Kemp but thass life ennit.

He and **Young Mal** *make noises of cars skidding.*

Rich   I wanna buy an ice cream, thass wat I meant.

Young Tone   Well go on then, ice cream van is still there.

Rich   Gimme my money then.

Young Tone *hands the change over.*

Rich   Wass this?

Young Tone   Yer money, unless yu don't wan it back.

Rich   It was two quid I gave yer.

Young Tone   Expenses.

Young Mal   I told yu not to lend him any. Yer so stupid.

Rich   This has to last me a week.

Young Mal   Stop yer crying.

Rich   I'm not cryin. I'm juss sayin. Wat am I supposed to do now?

Young Mal   Go down Soho be a rent boy.

Rich   Mal don't.

Young Tone   Yeah, yer outta order Mal.

Young Mal   I'm outta order?

Young Tone   Tellin him summin like that, how long we known him? Since primary school, thass how long. And all the thanks he gets is yu tellin him to be a rent boy, yer bad man.

Young Mal   Shut yer mum's legs.

Young Tone   Rich aint gonna be a rent boy.

Young Mal   Shut her little sister's legs.

Young Tone   He's too ugly, he can't even give it away.

Rich   Oh, ha ha my sides are achin'.

Young Tone   Yer face is gonna be achin'.

Rich   And yer whole body is gonna be bleedin' when that third year catches up wid yer.

Young Mal   Oh yeah, I fergot about him.

Young Tone   I ain't.

Young Mal   Shittin yerself Tone?

Young Tone   No.

Young Mal   I bet yu are.

Young Tone   I bet I ain't.

Young Mal   Stand up then.

Young Tone   No.

Rich   I bet he's drippin'.

Young Tone   Yu think yer so hard when yer wid him.

Rich   I know I am.

Young Mal   Go there Rich.

Young Tone   Yer nuttin. Yer mum is nuttin.

Rich   Shut up.

Young Tone   That third year is nuttin.

Young Mal   So yer gonna fight him then?

Young Tone   I ain't afraid.

Young Mal   Yu should be.

Young Tone   Why?

Young Mal   He's only got one eye.

Young Tone   Yer point?

Young Mal   His name's Terry Davies right, he's in the same class as my cousin Duane. He's a right nutter. He was fightin an older bloke outside school, wid knives – geezer cut his eye out.

Young Tone   So?

Young Mal   So he's hard.

Young Tone   No, it means the geezer who cut his eye out is hard, not him. I tell yer Mal, yer lettin me down.

Young Mal   Yer mum.

Young Tone   Tellin' us St George's is the hardest school. We're gonna get nuff respect!

Young Mal   It *is* the hardest school.

Young Tone   Yu told me it'll be a laugh wid all them black kids goin' there.

Young Mal   It will.

Young Tone   When?

Young Mal   Give it time awright. First day Duane went there, he saw one black kid beatin' up three white teachers.

Young Tone   Well it was our first day and we ain't seen nuttin.

Young Mal   Yu will.

Young Tone   Sure Duane weren't lyin'?

Young Mal   Duane don't lie right.

Rich   Ignore him Mal.

Young Mal   Shut up.

Young Tone   Maybe yer cousin aint as hard as yu say he is, maybe him and the rest of the St George's bwais are nuttin but pussies.

Young Mal   Yer mum's hole.

Young Tone   Yer granny's hole.

Young Mal   Rich, tell this fool whose door the police kicked down the oder week.

Rich   Yours.

Young Mal   And who did they come to arrest?

Rich   Duane.

Young Mal   Thank yu!

Young Tone   Oh I'm so impressed. Rich, tell this fool whose door the police kicked down on Saturday.

Rich   Yours.

Young Tone   Who did they come to arrest?

Rich   Yer dad.

Young Tone   Thank yu. Now tell him as well whose door they kicked down yesterday.

Rich   Yours again!

Young Tone   Who were they lookin for?

Rich   Yer dad's brother.

Young Tone   Thank yu!

Young Mal   How many times yer dad's brother bin stopped by the police then? None. How many times my cousin? Untold!

Young Tone   How many times yu bin stopped by the police? None!

Young Mal   Once.

Young Tone   Yer mum.

Young Mal   KFC, High Street Ken. They said I looked like sum kid who was shopliftin' in Mister Byrite.

Young Tone   Mister Byrite? Yer tramp!

Young Mal   Wat about yu then?

Young Tone   Three times.

Young Mal   Lie.

Young Tone   Shame, shame, take the blame.

Young Mal   Why they stoppin yu?

Young Tone   Ca' I'm a bad bwai!

Young Mal   Yer a mummy's bwai.

Young Tone   Yu think yer so hard cos yer black.

Young Mal   We are.

Young Tone   (*at* **Rich**) Him! (*Laughs.*)

Young Mal   Yu juss wait.

Young Tone   I'm waitin'.

Young Mal   I'll take yu now.

Young Tone   Come now if yer bad.

Rich   Don't.

Young Mal   Don't get stressed Rich.

Young Tone   This ain't gonna take long.

Young Mal   No time at all.

The boys arm-wrestle. **Young Tone** *gets the upper hand pushing* **Young Mal** *to the ground.*

Young Tone   I'm blacker than yu Mal!

Young Mal   Yer wish. (*Falls to the floor.*)

Young Tone   Winner!

Young Mal *pulls* **Young Tone** *down. They roll around on the floor.*

Young Tone   Oh yes, Bruno's back on form. He's throwin sum weighty punches here, but wait, Tyson's on the attack now, he clips him, he clips him again. Bruno is in real trouble now, this will soon be over.

Rich   Get off him.

Young Tone   Anoder clip!

Rich   Leave him!

Young Tone   Now Bonecrusher Smith wants a go. Tyson clips him, and again, and again, and again . . .

Rich   Stop it, get off, get off, get off me Dad!

Young Tone   Wat?

Rich   Juss leave me.

Young Tone   Did yu call me Dad? He did didn't he?

Rich   I don't like it.

Young Tone   Wat yu cryin' for? It was a joke.

Rich   I ain't cryin'.

Young Tone   Yeah!

Young Mal   We're juss muckin' about Rich.

Young Tone   Callin' me Dad.

Young Mal   Yu awright Rich?

Rich   Yeah.

Young Mal   Yu made any planes today Rich? I bet yu have. Show us.

Rich *shows him.*

Young Mal   Smart man. (*Flies it.*) See that? Right across the playground.

Young Tone   Yer farts go across the playground.

Young Mal   Make us on, and one for Tone.

Rich (*rips out more paper*)   I'm glad we're at St George's.

Young Mal   Ennit.

Rich   I don't miss Avondale at all. Mum wanted me to go Burlington Danes. Seen their uniform? All green.

Young Mal   Seen their girls? Rough!

Young Tone   I'm juss glad I don't have to sit next to Danny Kemp no more.

The boys make skidding car noises again.

Young Mal   I'd rather sit next to Danny Kemp than Lisa Davies. Seen her face? Come like a pizza.

Young Tone   Yu wanna shag her.

Young Mal   Fuck off Tone!

Rich   Girls are shit.

Young Mal/Young Tone   Ennit!

Rich   Ready?

The boys aim the planes.

One, two, three – lift off!

The boys fly the planes.

Young Mal   Yessir!

Young Tone   Not as fast as mine dough.

Young Mal   Shut up, mine topped yours easy. Take it like a man Tone.

Rich   I'll get them. Yu should be mekin these yerself. (*Exits.*)

Young Mal   We're no good dough. Yer the best Rich, yu know that.

Young Tone   He did call me Dad. Yu tellin me yu didn't hear him?

Young Mal   It don't matter.

Young Tone   I hope he aint gonna be like that all year man, he's gonna bring us down.

Young Mal   Juss leave him.

Young Tone   Yeah awright. I mean St George's is a pussy school anyway.

Young Mal   Yu wait till Wednesday.

Young Tone   Wass appenin?

Young Mal   A whole heap of Duane's year are gonna fight Holland Park.

Young Tone   Lie.

Young Mal   True. His mate Delroy is leadin' it. Nuff fights.

Young Tone   Yu goin'?

Young Mal   Course.

Young Tone   And me.

Young Mal   Delroy told me if I do awright, he's gonna let me join his crew.

Young Tone   Yeah?

Young Mal   Yep.

Young Tone   Mal?

Young Mal   Wat?

Young Tone   (*pleads*) Help me join his crew as well.

The same kids' playground. Ten years later.

Mal *and* **Tone**, *now in their early twenties, are sharing a spliff.*

Mal (*mimics*)   'Mal, help me join his crew as well.' That was yu.

Tone (*gives him the finger*)   Why remember that?

Mal   Cos I bloody want to. Yu a copper or summin?

Tone   Yu remember then I could mash yu up.

Mal   Yu wanna try it now Tone, come!

Tone   Did I say that? Did those words leave my lips?

Mal   They wouldn't. Don't bum suck it.

Tone   I weren't.

Mal   Looks like yer pissed on it man.

Tone   Aint even that good.

Mal   Don't even go deh right. Yu know how much I paid for this?

Tone   My money too, so swivel.

Mal Well pardon fuckin me yer majesty.

Tone Yer majesty? I like that.

Mal Let's see how yu like it wid my trainer up yer arse. (*He takes a drag and starts coughing.*) Fuck! This is shit.

Tone Told yer. Ware d'yu get it from?

Mal Spencer.

Tone Yu told me he aint nuttin but a piss-taker.

Mal He is.

Tone So why buy weed off him then?

Mal Grant weren't around.

Tone I don't feel high or nuttin.

Mal He's touched me up ennit?

Tone Yer such a fool Mal.

Mal Bastard! BASTARD! I swear to God Tone, it's the last time I ever do business wid a nigger.

Tone (*laughs*) Wat?

Mal I'm serious. Nuttin but cunts man.

Tone Yu can't say that.

Mal Why?

Tone Yer black ennit.

Mal Yu know how long I was waitin' outside the tube station for Spencer to show his ugly face? An hour! Guy carries on like I got no life. Pisses me off man. When he finally shows, I ask ware he's bin, so he start givin me all de chat – 'Wa 'appenin' nuh man? Ease up nuh. Wat de rass, me say me soon come, so me here. Is why yu get stress? Come like a white man, backside!'

Tone *howls with laughter.*

Mal   I goes, 'Get the fuck outta my face wid that shit
Spencer, ware's my ting?' He acts like he juss come off the
plane from Jamaica. Jamaica! He lives in bloody Clapham –
never bin abroad in his life. I was this much away from
cuttin him yu nuh? Wait will I see him next. Niggers. Least
white guys don't fuck about wid yu, yu wid me?

Tone   Watever man.

Mal   Yu say half seven, they're there at half seven.
Sumtimes they're there at seven. Keen or wat! Every time I
see Grant, it's all, 'Awright mate, how's it goin'? Sweet as a
nut. Got the dosh for me? Nice one. Here's yer gear, smoke
one for me yeah. (*Sings.*) No woman no cry . . . Anyhows
must dash, bitta business up west, know wat I mean? Be
lucky!' See wat I mean? Stop bloody laughin'.

Tone   But yer funny man. Yu come like Eddie Murphy.

Mal   I'm serious Tone. Awright, next time yu buy the shit
off Spencer, yu'll see wat I'm chattin' about then.

Tone   Awright Grandad.

A mobile phone rings. Both boys search their pockets.

Mal (*smug*)   Mine.

Tone   Suck my dick.

Mal (*answers*)   Yeah who dis? Awright man, wass up?

Tone   Who is it?

Mal   Wat? Nuh man, I'm not up for it dread.

Tone   Who is it?

Mal   Not tonight man, ca' I'm busy.

Tone   Who is it, who is it?

Mal   Will yu fuck off! (*To phone.*) Na Teddy, not yu man.
Juss a piece of turd that love to aggravate me.

Tone   Wass he want?

Mal   Hold up yeah. (*To Tone.*) He wants to link up tonight, sum flat he wants to do over in Chelsea. Yu happy now?

Tone   Cool.

Mal   Who invited yu?

Tone   Oh come on man.

Mal   Sorry Teddy.

Tone   Come on.

Mal   Anoder time yeah.

Tone   Yu ain't busy Mal.

Mal   I am right.

Tone   I ain't, don't blow it for me.

Mal (*to phone*)   Yu asked Tone? Tony Vincent, hangs round wid me, white guy. (*Laughs.*) Yeah yeah thass the one. (*Howls.*) Oh no, na yer bad man.

Tone   Wat yu laughin' at?

Mal   He's safe man, he is Teddy, trust me yeah. Awright, laters. Yer bad man. (*Hangs up.*) Yer in. He'll check yu later.

Tone   Wass he say about me?

Mal   It don't matter.

Tone   Tell me.

Mal   It don't matter man.

Tone   Why don't yu wanna come?

Mal   I wanna night off. Is that allowed?

Tone   Yu seein' a woman?

Mal   Maybe.

Tone   Who?

Mal   Don't worry about it.

Tone   How come yer phone always rings but not mine?

Mal   Cos yu stink.

Tone   Six bloody weeks I've had this, not one bastard's rung me.

Mal   I have.

Tone   Yu don't count. Yu sold me it.

Mal   So?

Tone   So how come it don't work.

Mal   The phone works fine right so shut up. Ain't my fault yu got no friends.

Tone   Suck my dick.

Mal   Fuck yer mum.

Tone   Yer rass. Wat did Teddy say about me?

Mal (*clips him*)   Shut up man, yer goin' wid him, be happy.

Tone   Don't mess up my hair Mal.

Mal   Or wat?

Tone   I bus' yer head.

Mal   Come nuh?

Tone   Who yu seein' tonight?

Mal   Don't worry about it?

Tone   Is it Nicole?

Mal   Yu mad! I ain't goin out wid that slag.

Tone   Yu gave her one dough.

Mal   That don't make me hers.

Tone   I saw her the other day, she was askin' after yu. I reckon she's still up for it.

Mal   Yu've never had a girl in yer life yu virgin . . . (*Holds his nose as it starts to bleed.*)

Tone   Rah man, yu awright?

Mal   Yeah yeah I'm fine. Stop starin' at me.

Tone   Juss don't bleed on my trainers right. Yu know how much these cost?

Mal   I'm awright.

Tone   Yeah looks it, yer invalid.

Mal   Juss gimme a minute.

Tone   I wanna go down the pub dough.

Mal   Go on then. Tone?

Tone   Yo?

Mal   Stick wid me tonight?

Tone   Thought yu weren't comin.

Mal   I changed my mind. Stick wid me in case there's trouble.

Tone   It's juss a flat we're doin'.

Mal   Yu don't know Teddy like I do, first sign of grief and he's the one shittin' himself.

Tone   Teddy's a spa man.

Mal   He's an arsehole. Stay close I'll get yu out.

Tone   Yu my mum or summin?

Mal   I feel I am half the time. (*His nose starts to bleed again.*) Shit!

Tone   Yu got a leak? Wass the matter wid yer?

Mal (*snaps*)   Nuttin!

Tone's bedroom.

Tone *is alone watching a porno video.* **Carol** *enters, dressed in school uniform.*

Carol   How bout yu turn it up a bit Tone, I don't think the next street can hear ya . . .

Tone   Yu mind?

Carol   No.

Tone   Yu never knock.

Carol   Shut up man. Wat yu watchin'?

Tone   (*Switches the television off with his remote.*) Do yer homework.

Carol   Done it.

Tone   Ware's Davey?

Carol   In the livin' room, screamin' his stupid head off.

Tone   Well look after him then.

Carol   Yu look after him, he's yer brother as well yer nuh. (*Grabs the remote, turns the television on.*) Wat yu watchin?

Tone   Carol!

Carol   Fuck! Is that real?

Tone   Gimme my remote.

Carol   Size of his dick man.

Tone   Yu got a nasty mout.

Carol   Oh swivel.

Tone (*holds out his hand for the remote*)   Give.

He switches the channel over. **Carol** *presses the remote.* **Tone** *switches the channel over again. This escalates until* **Tone** *turns the television off altogether.*

Carol   Yer such a dry one ennit?

Tone   Get outta my face.

Carol   Yu think I don't know about them *Penthouses* yu got hidden under yer bed, yer perv!

Tone   Wat yu doin' lookin' under my bed – wat yu doin' in my room?

Carol   Awright don't get vex, I wanted to borrow one of yer CDs.

Tone   Keep outta my bloody room.

Carol   Yes buana! (*Turns the television back on.*)

Tone   Yu don't stop do yu? Yer like a fly I can't swat.

Carol   I'm bored.

Tone   Thass not my problem.

Carol   I've seen better ones than this anyway.

Tone   Ware?

Carol   Linsey's broder got a whole box of them. Me and her were watchin them one time havin' a right laugh.

Tone   I'm gonna be havin' words with Linsey's broder. (*Turns the television off again.*)

Carol   He'd beat the shit outta yu.

Tone   Yu reckon?

Carol   I know.

Tone   I've had him before right.

Carol   When yu were five?

Tone   When we were at a rave a couple years back. He tells me I'm tryin to move in on his gal, he starts pushin' me, shoutin' the odds. I pull my blade – yu shoulda seen how fast he run.

Carol   Was that before or after he went to prison?

Tone   Before.

Carol   Don't count then.

Tone   Wat yu mean it don't count.

Carol   Yu seen him lately? He's bin pumpin' iron. Chest come like Usher. Yu best let Mal deal wid him.

Tone   I don't need Mal for everything.

Carol   No one's fitter than Mal. Tone, I ain't see him lately, is he awright?

Tone   Wat yu mean?

Carol   Nuttin, I'm juss askin' is he awright, yer spas.

Tone   He's fine.

Carol   Good.

Tone   Yer droolin' on my floor Carol.

Carol   Move.

Tone   Like Mal's gonna go for a little kid like yu.

Carol   I ain't a kid right.

Tone   Still talkin' to him in yer sleep? 'Oh Mal, kiss me Mal, kiss me . . .'

Carol   Fuck off.

Tone   Yu fuck off.

Carol   Gimme a fag.

Tone   No.

Carol   Tightarse. (*Turns the television on.*) Rah man, wass he doin to her now?

Tone   Don't yu know?

Carol   I fergot.

Tone   Yu don't know.

Carol   Awright smartarse, yu tell me.

Tone   I will.

Carol   Go on then.

Tone   Sixty-nine.

Carol *laughs.*

Tone   Wat yu laughin at?

Carol   Sixty-nine? Newsflash Tone, that ain't a sixty-nine.

Tone   It is.

Carol   It ain't. Aah, yer goin' all red now. Its awright don't worry about it Tone.

Tone   Worry about wat?

Carol   Juss admit it.

Tone   I ain't admittin' nuttin.

Carol   Yu don't know wat a sixty-nine is.

Tone   I do.

Carol   It ain't hard to work out yer nuh? (*Draws the number 69 in the air.*) Six, nine! Man and woman lyin' down on top of each other, her arse in his face, yu need a picture?

Tone   Get out.

Carol   Hold up. (*Fast-forwards the film.*) There's always one sumware. There! (*Puts the film on pause.*) Thass a sixty-nine. Got it?

Tone (*turns the television off*)   Touch the television again and I'll bus' yer head.

Carol   No wonder yu can't get a gal of yer own.

Tone   I can get any gal I want.

Carol   Yeah right.

Tone   Carol, do yu see me goin' into yer room?

Carol   Can if yu like, I don't care.

Tone   See yu and yer bloody Boyzone posters?

Carol   Boyzone! I gotta life mate.

Tone   Juss piss off right.

Carol   It's only cos I care Tone. Yer my big brother. Yu shouldn't be watchin' these, it's not normal.

Tone   So how come yu and Linsey watch them?

Carol   Yeah but we're girls dough, it's different. It ain't the same with us. Blokes who watch these have got bigger tits than mine Tone.

Tone   Yu think yer tits are big?

Carol   Oh funny. (*Finds a Walkman.*) Ware yu get this?

Tone   For fuck's sake.

Carol   Juss let me look at it man. It's smart. (*Plays the Walkman and dances around the room.*)

Tone (*watches his sister in disbelief*)   Get off.

Carol   Show me sum moves man.

Tone   Get off me.

Carol   I'm bored Tone.

Tone   I don't care. Look at yer – come like Linsey every day man.

Carol   Yer point?

Tone   She's a slapper.

Carol   Linsey ain't no slapper.

Tone   She's shagged nuff men.

Carol   She ain't shagged yu.

Tone   I wouldn't touch her wid Mal's.

Carol   Mal's awready had her.

Tone   Wat?

Carol   Aah, ain't he told yer? Well she told me. Best she's ever had man.

Tone   Fuck off wid yer shit.

Carol   It's true. She likes her meat burnt ennit?

Tone   Yu ain't seein' her from now on, right?

Carol   Quiet horse.

Tone   Sit on yer arse and do yer homework.

Carol   I'm goin' out right and I'm pullin' a bloke.

Tone   Who's gonna touch yu?

Carol   I've had loads of guys touchin' me.

Tone   Yer a virgin Carol, so shut yer mout.

Carol   Ain't.

Tone   Are.

Carol   I ain't.

Tone   Yu bloody are.

Carol   Least I know wat a sixty-nine is.

Tone *jerks his fist like he's going to hit her.*

Carol   Yeah? And at least Linsey shares her fags wid me, unlike sum people. She's gonna let me be one of her sisters man!

Tone *grunts.*

Carol   She is right. She go do up my hair, gimme sum make-up, wear one of her dresses. Gonna get me a man Tone, a big black sexy fit man. Wat yu laughin' for? It's good enough for Mum it's good enough for me. She thinks I'm ugly.

Tone   Who?

Carol   Mum. I heard her sayin' it to Mal's mum. 'Carol's so plain, Carol's so borin', she never goes out, jus' stays in with the telly.' I never go out cos she won't let me, the two-faced bitch.

Tone   Oi!

Carol   Oh shut up, I've heard yu say worse. Well I'm gonna bloody show her now man, and yu.

Tone *grabs the Walkman off* **Carol**.

Carol   Yer such an old woman.

Tone   (*his mobile phone rings*) Oh man yes! Yes man!

Carol   Yu never heard a phone go off before?

Tone   I ain't heard mine go off before. See that light flashin' – look, look! They wanna speak to me, Tone bwai! Me, Carol.

Carol   Well answer it then.

Tone   Let me enjoy the sound man.

Carol   Ware yu nick it?

Tone   I don't tief everything I own right, I bought it off Mal.

Carol   Wid money? Yu actually went out and earned sum money?

Tone   No I nicked the money.

Carol   So in a way yu did tief it.

Tone   No I said – juss shut up. (*Phone stops ringing.*) That was yer fault. I won't know who it is now. Yu can't stop chattin' into my face can yer?

Carol   Go change yer nappy bwai!

Tone   Yu best pray they call back right. (*He waits. And waits. Phone rings.*) Who dis? Yeah? Teddy! Yeah wass up man?

Carol (*messing about*)   Oh Tone, don't stop Tone, put it back in Tone, give it to me Tone, right there, right there oooh Tone, Tone!

Tone   Wat? Na juss sum girl, can't get enough of me ennit? Yeah, yeah I'm ready man.

Carol   Come on Tone, oh, oh, oh . . . (*Shouts.*) Yes, yes Tone!

Tone   I'm comin' now. (*Hangs up.*) Yer sick.

Carol   I deserve a thank yu actually.

Tone   Fuck off.

Carol   He'll respect yu now ennit? He'll think yu got pussy on the go. Him tink yu is a bad bwai! (*Gives him a nudge.*)

Tone   Get off.

Carol *gives him another nudge.*

Tone   Carol!

Carol *goes to give her brother another nudge, but before she can* **Tone** *grabs her. He tickles her ruthlessly.* **Carol** *laughs out loud.* **Tone** *lets her go.*

Carol   Bastard!

Tone   Laters.

Carol   Let me come.

Tone   Yer babysittin'.

Carol   I'm aways babysittin', I'm bor . . .

Tone (*finishes*)   . . . bored! Don't even think about goin' out right.

Carol   I wouldn't do that. Especially if my nice handsome older brother let me play sum tunes.

Tone   If I said no you'll juss come in anyway.

Carol   No!

Tone   Yer such a liar. Don't touch nuttin' else right.

Carol   Cheers broth. Run along then.

Tone *exits.* **Carol** *plays some tunes and dances around the room. She doesn't notice* **Tone** *coming back in. He sneaks up behind her and tickles her.* **Carol** *jumps,* **Tone** *runs out laughing.*

Carol   Sod!

The kids' playground.

Mal *is alone downstage smoking a cigarette.* **Young Mal** *and* **Rich** *are on the monkey bars making paper aeroplanes.*

Young Mal   Guess wat? I was sittin' next to Lisa Davies in maths today

Rich   Yu always sit next to her.

Young Mal   Her tits are gettin' bigger.

Rich   Errgh!

Young Mal   Wat yu mean errgh? Yer queer.

Rich   I ain't a queer.

Young Mal   Why say errgh then?

Rich   Cos it's Lisa Davies, yu used to call her a dog.

Young Mal   Well she ain't no dog now.

Rich   She is.

Young Mal   She's lookin' good.

Rich   She ain't.

Young Mal   She had lipstick on.

Rich   She's still a dog.

Young Mal   She had one of her shirt buttons undone, she's wearin' a bra now.

Rich   Shut up.

Young Mal   Look at her tomorrow Rich, yu tellin' me yu wouldn't fuck her?

Rich   Yeah.

Young Mal   Queer.

Rich   Don't call me that.

Young Mal   Yer the one who said yu didn't wanna screw her.

Rich   I don't fancy her. Thass all.

Young Mal   Queer.

Rich   I mean it Mal.

Young Mal   Yu wanna fight me Rich?

Rich   No.

Young Mal   Yu look well scary when yu get like that.

Rich (*looking at Mal's aeroplane*)   Yer doin' it wrong. Get it right will yer.

Young Mal   If yu don't fancy Lisa, who then?

Rich   Who says I have to fancy anyone?

Young Mal   I say. Tone fancies someone.

Rich   Who?

Young Mal   Miss Gordon.

Rich   She's a teacher, she's well old.

Young Mal   At least he fancies someone.

Rich   Jenny Charles!

Young Mal   Jenny Charles? Yu never said nuttin' before.

Rich   Is that against the law?

Young Mal   She's cute – fat but cute. Yu want me to ask her out for yer?

Rich   No.

Young Mal   Go on.

Rich   I said no.

Young Mal   Yu don't fancy Jenny Charles, yu juss said the first name that came into yer head.

Rich   I do fancy her, thass ware yer wrong. I think about her all the time Mal, so shame!

Young Mal   Ask her out then.

Rich   I can't.

Young Mal   Wat yu mean yu can't?

Rich   I dunno, I juss can't.

Young Mal   Loner.

Rich   I reckon she likes me as well.

Young Mal   So get in there.

Rich   She always says hello, she walked right across the playground to do it once.

Young Mal   So get in there Rich.

Rich   How can she fancy me dough?

Young Mal   Wass wrong wid yu?

Rich   (*points to his chin*) Chinny! It's wat all yu call me ennit?

Young Mal   Yu love to feel sorry for yerself don't yer?

Rich   Yu love to run me down.

Young Mal   Yu wanna slap?

Rich   Yu take the piss outta me.

Young Mal   Juss shut up. Yu fancy her right?

Rich   I don't know.

Young Mal   Yu juss said yu did. Ask the bloody girl out Rich, I'm not jokin wid yer. Yu wanna be a loner all yer life?

Rich   I'm not a loner.

Young Mal   Yes yu are. And I'm a bloody loner as well for hangin' out wid yer. Why d'yer think Tone isn't hangin' round wid us? He's got better things to do than fly stupid aeroplanes man.

Rich   My planes ain't stupid right.

Young Mal   He's hangin' round wid Delroy's gang, the only white kid there man. That ain't right. And yu know wat Delroy said to me, if we ain't better than white kids we ain't nuttin'.

Rich   Well piss off then, go away.

Young Mal   Awright I will, yu little queer.

Rich *throws a punch.* **Mal** *falls.*

Rich (*climbs down*)   Yu awright Mal? Mal? I'm sorry awright. Yu OK?

Young Mal (*jumps up*)   Yu punch hard ennit? I tell yer man, if yu carried on like that, nuff kids would be scared of yu – even Delroy. Jenny would think yer hard as well.

Rich   Leave me alone.

Young Mal   We can hang round wid Delroy. Come on Rich.

Rich   Yu never listen to me.

Young Mal   Listen to wat, wat yu sayin?

Rich   I don't wanna do it.

Young Mal   Wass yer problem?

Rich   I don't wanna be like my dad awright?

Young Mal   Thought so. Yeah well yer mad. If I had a dad like yours, I'd be well proud. See anyone messin' wid him?

Rich   I had a row wid my mum las' night, yu know wat she said to me?

Young Mal   Shut up about yer mum.

Rich   She goes, every time I get angry or upset I look juss like Dad. It's like she's scared of me as well now.

Young Mal   Rich!

Rich   No! I don't wanna be like him, I don't wanna be like any of them right. And yu can't make me.

Young Mal   Shut up. Why yu love to take things seriously? Yer so heavy. All I want yu to do is show that yer hard for fuck's sake.

Rich   Why?

Young Mal   It's the only way to be man. Show yer temper a bit more, prove yer hard. Yu hear wat I said?

Rich   Yes.

Young Mal   And I'll help yer. Yu and me yeah? Yeah? Rich?

Rich   Awright, juss don't go on.

Young Mal   Smile then.

Rich *puts on a false smile.*

Young Mal   Don't strain yerself.

Rich   I gotta go in.

Young Mal   Yeah, and me. Race yu up?

Rich   Na.

Young Mal   Come on.

Rich   I got a dead leg.

Young Mal   Juss to the first floor then. Don't be so borin' Rich.

Rich   Awright.

Young Mal   I count to three yeah.

The boys get into starting positions.

One, two! (*He runs off on two. Exits.*)

Rich   Mal! We run on three, not two.

Young Mal (*offstage*)   Come on then!

Rich   Yu bloody cheat! (*Looks towards the older* **Mal**.) Yu aways did that.

Mal   Yu aways fell for it. (*Feels his stare.*) Wat? Wat! I ain't sayin' sorry to yer.

Rich   I'm not askin' yu to.

Mal   I warned yu. Didn't yu hear me? Juss go awright.

Rich   Yer scared Mal.

Mal   Scared of wat?

Rich   Yu know wat.

Mal   Juss move.

Rich   Wat yu worryin' for?

Mal   Who's worryin'?

Rich   Yu might be awright.

Mal   Yu turn deaf?

Rich   How much yu wanna bet yu'll be awright?

Mal   Juss leave me alone man.

Rich *offers him the plane.*

Mal   I don't want it.

Rich   I bet yu ain't even told Tone – yer spa!

Mal   There's nuttin' to tell.

Rich   I know wat yer feelin'.

Mal   Yu don't know shit.

Tone *comes running on, shouting.*

Rich   Tell him Mal, tell him. *(Walks past* **Tone** *as he exits.)*

Tone   *(without seeing him)* Yu wanna go? Come now! Come now!

Mal   Tone, wat yu doin?

Tone   Get off the bus and come here!

Mal   Who yu shoutin' at man?

Tone   Wanker of a bus conductor. Threw me off the bus. Yeah, run yer lickle rass yu, run! *(To* **Mal**.*)* Coulda backed me up.

Mal   Shut up.

Tone   Coulda helped me bus' him head.

Mal   And get done? Why he throw yu off?

Tone   I was havin' a laugh.

Mal   Yu were fuckin' about.

Tone   I was on the bus right, I show him my pass, I sneak it back to Teddy cos he got no money, the bastard catches us, and gets all stressed. Cunt!

Mal   Teddy can't pay up for once in his life.

Tone   He had no money, yu deaf?

Mal   How much was it, 80p? Yu couldn't lend him?

Tone   Wat for? We're havin' a laugh man, guy got no sense of humour.

Mal   Yu ain't twelve any more Tone, wass the matter wid yu?

Tone   Oh man shut up. Jesus, yu come like my mum.

Mal   Yer pissed.

Tone   Loner!

Mal   Yu high?

Tone   No.

Mal   Keep still then.

Tone   I am.

Mal   This is keepin' still?

Tone   Yu turn policeman now?

Mal   How many yu had?

Tone   Had?

Mal   E's.

Tone   Couple. Grant weren't around. Yu told me not to deal wid a nigger, so I checked sum white guys who were drinkin down the Sussex.

Mal   Wat yu doin' goin' in there?

Tone   I told yer, Grant weren't around.

Mal   Stupid white wankers drink in there Tone, yu wanna be like them?

Tone   I am like them dough, so I must be a wanker right? Wat, yu gonna laugh now? Go on, I don't care, ca' I've had it man, yu lot laughin' at me.

Mal   Yu ever see me laughin' at yu?

Tone   Teddy calls me a fuckin' wigger.

Mal   Teddy's a spas.

Tone   Tellin' me his bamboo is longer than mine.

Mal   Wat are yu chattin' about?

Tone   We went for a piss in the park. I see his ting, he tells me his is bigger than mine, but it ain't. He laughs at me Mal, he bloody laughed. His ting ain't that big – thicker, but not bigger. His swings to the left, I know cos he pissed on my trainers. And he tries and denies it. At least mine's in the middle, I can shoot straight. He juss laughs man. I saw yours once, it weren't big either Mal or thick, juss average. None of yer lot are bigger right, we're all the bloody same! But he juss keeps laughin' man.

Mal   Wat yu want me to say Tone? Yer dick is the same as mine.

Tone   Yeah, go on then.

Mal   Fine then, watever. In fact, yer dick's bigger than mine.

Tone   Yeah?

Mal   T-rex size.

Tone   Yer juss tryin' to mek me feel better.

Mal   Get yer dick out.

Tone   Excuse me?

Mal   Get it out.

Tone   Is yer name Melinda Messenger?

Mal   I'll get mine out.

Tone   Yu on the turn or summin?

Mal   Yours is bigger Tone, let's prove it right now.

Tone   It's broad daylight man.

Mal   Yeah, I suppose yer right. Yu couldn't see mine anyway, it's so small. When we were at school, I used to look at yours.

Tone   Did yer?

Mal   Yeah.

Tone   Why?

Mal   It was hard not to. Yu nearly knocked me over with it.

Tone   Yeah?

Mal   Yeah.

Tone   How come yu never said nuttin?

Mal   Wat yu expect me to say? 'Bredren, check out Tone's piece, shame us all!' I was jealous. So, how's it feel?

Tone   Awright.

Mal   Wear tighter jeans, show it off more, get nuff pussy. Wat?

Tone   Did yu fuck Linsey?

Mal   Linsey? Ferget that slag man.

Tone   Did yu dough?

Mal   Wass it matter?

Tone   Yu never said.

Mal   Wass it matter?

Tone   Every time I try and mek moves on her, she don't wanna know, like I'm shit.

Mal   Ferget her, she was a lousy fuck anyway. Yu got a third leg man, be happy.

Tone   Yu have got a bigger dick. Nuff gals fancy yu. Even my little sister's up for it now.

Mal   Bloody hell Tone, yer so fuckin' helpless.

Tone   Help me then!

Mal   Wid wat? Yu carry on like there's sum big magic secret.

Tone   Well there must be.

Mal   There ain't.

Tone   Yer lyin'.

Mal   Will yu listen to me.

Tone   No.

Mal (*blurts it out*)   Tone I'm sick!

Tone   Watcha say?

Mal (*unable to finish the sentence*)   . . . and tired. I'm sick and tired. I'm juss sick and tired of this shit awright. I juss am.

Tone   Wa gwan man? All I want is to be yu man and yer givin' me this shit.

Mal   Ferget it.

Tone   Ain't my fault I think yer brilliant. And yu are brilliant. Tellin' yu, yu juss, yer juss brilliant, an' I love yu man, big time, I love yu.

Mal (*laughs*)   Come here. (*Grabs his friend, holds him playfully in a headlock.*) Say that again and I'll deck yer. Wat yu like?

Tone   All I wanna be is like yu.

Mal   Yu mean yu wanna fuck a girl.

Tone   Well I ain't queer.

Mal   Yu really wanna fuck.

Tone   Yeah I really wanna fuck.

Mal   Come then let's go. Come!

Tone   Ware?

Mal   Subterrania.

Tone   We got chucked outta there.

Mal   We'll go West End then. Bar Rumba, Limelight or summin. Mal junior is gonna get sum action tonight, cos wat yu said was right. I am the fittest, and I always will be. And yer gonna get sum tonight, for the first time Tone, I promise yer. Wass my name Tone?

Tone   Mal.

Mal   Ennit.

Blackout.

Part Two

The kids' playground.

Young Tone   Bastard, I'll cut yu up right!

Young Mal   Awright Tone.

Young Tone   Yu don't say nuttin' about my mum.

Young Mal   Wat about yu then? Tellin' him his mum shags dogs.

Young Tone   Don't mean he can say wat he likes about my mum. (*To* **Rich**.) Cos yu can't right.

Young Mal (*to* **Rich**)   Yu juss gonna let him do this? Fight him man!

Rich   Piss off. (*Exits.*)

Young Tone   Yeah run, yu batay bwai! Who's he think he is, callin' my mum a slag.

Young Mal   She is dough ain't she? Wat? Yu wanna start on me Tone? Yu still think yu can beat me up, come on then!

Young Tone   I don't want sum loner sayin' it dough.

Young Mal   Shut up.

Young Tone   We ain't at primary school now.

Young Mal   Wat yu tellin me for?

Young Tone   He's yer mate.

Young Mal   Yu knew him first.

Young Tone   He calls my mum a slag again he's dead right.

Young Mal   If he really wanted to Tone, he could beat the shit outta yu.

Young Tone   Why, cos he's black? I bet yu wanna go after him, kiss and make up.

Young Mal   Shut yer mum's legs.

Young Tone   Fool's only left his bag ain't he? (*Rifles through, finds a plane.*) See wat I mean?

Young Mal   Thass his swift. Don't look at me like that, it's wat he calls it.

Young Tone   So it was yu Delroy saw.

Young Mal   Saw wat?

Young Tone   Yu on the school roof wid Chinny yesterday, flyin off bloody planes.

Young Mal   Yer mum.

Young Tone   Yu callin' Delroy a liar?

Young Mal   No.

Young Tone   So it was yu?

Young Mal   No.

Young Tone   Rich is bringin' yu down Mal.

Young Mal   I can dump him anytime I like right.

Young Tone   Yeah.

Young Mal   Watch me.

Young Tone   Delroy's gonna call yu nuff names Mal, he's gonna make everyone call yu them. I'll have to say them.

Young Mal   Yu can try.

Young Tone   Yu aways think I'm shit. I ain't the one hangin' round wid a loner right.

Young Mal   I ain't hangin' round wid him.

Rich *enters.*

Rich   I fergot my bag.

Young Mal   Take it then.

Young Tone   I'm off.

Young Mal   Ware yu goin'?

Young Tone   Checkin' Delroy.

Young Mal   Come let's go then.

Young Tone   Who invited yu? Yu stay wid yer girlfriend.

Young Mal   Yu wanna die?

Young Tone   Laters. (*Laughs as he exits.*)

Young Mal   Don't yu listen Rich?

Rich   I did wat yu said.

Young Mal   I told yu to say, '*and* yer mum'. Yu don't call his mum a slag right out.

Rich   (*mimics*) 'And yer mum, and yer dad, and yer gran, cha blood clart!'

Young Mal   Don't tek the piss. Yu said yu'll try.

Rich   I did try, and I still hate it. Ware yer goin'?

Young Mal   I'm gonna check Delroy.

Rich   I'm gonna fly my swift off the balcony dough.

Young Mal   Oh yu fuckin' loner!

Rich   Mal?

Young Mal   I ain't got time for yu right. (*Exits.*)

Night-bus stop in Trafalgar Square.

Mal *is with* **Hannah**.

Mal   Ware yu goin' again?

Hannah   Brixton.

Mal (*checks timetable*)   Yu got a long wait.

Hannah   Then I'll wait.

Mal   Well don't yu worry about a ting right Hannah.

Hannah   Who's worried?

Mal   We'll keep yu company yeah, make sure yu don't hassled and that.

Hannah   Do you mind?

Mal   It's only me hand.

Hannah   I know it's your hand, just keep it to yourself please.

Mal   Yu wanna feel summin else?

Hannah (*disgusted*)   Oh God.

Mal   Chill.

Hannah   Get off me!

Mal   Wass yer problem?

Hannah   I ain't got a problem, you seem to have a problem with your hands though.

Mal   Awright gal, ease up.

Hannah   I'm not your gal.

Mal   Yer so ungrateful yu know that? We're not the ones who left yu on yer own.

Hannah (*insincere*)   Gee Mal, thanks! Just stay where you are.

Tone *enters with bags of KFC.*

Tone   Food!

Mal   Yu had to kill the chicken yerself or summin?

Tone   There was a long queue.

Mal   Fuck the queue juss barge in man. Well chuck it over. 'Kin 'ell.

The boys dive into their food and chomp away.

Tone (*with his mouth full*)   Sure yu don't want any?

Hannah   I'm sure.

Tone   There's plenty.

Hannah   I'll survive.

Mal (*holds up his burger*)   Yu mind tellin' me wat this is?

Tone   Tower Burger.

Mal   And yer mum. Yu call this a bitta chicken? One bite thass it. Yu didn't check in the box?

Tone   They juss bunged them in and gimme them.

Mal   Always check the box Tone! Them Africans love to take the piss.

Tone   I got loads of fries.

Mal   I don't want nonna yer fries, I want chicken.

Tone   Ware yer goin?

Mal   To throw this shit back in their face. 'Bout Tower Burger – I wanna a big fuck-off chicken breast wid mayonnaise Tower Burger in my stomach before I go to bed yu understand me? They fuckin' wouldn't have done it if it were me right.

Tone   Bet yu come back wid niche.

Mal   Watch me now. (*Exits.*)

Tone   Gwan Mal!

Hannah   Is he on something?

Tone   Don't fuck wid a bwai and him chicken.

Hannah   He ain't all there.

Tone   He's awright.

Hannah   You know eating with your mouth closed won't kill you.

Tone   Ware yu goin' again?

Hannah   Brixton.

Tone   Got a long wait.

Hannah   I know!

Tone   Yu should give yer friend a slap when yu see her next.

Hannah   I will don't worry.

Tone   Leavin yu in the club alone so she can get off wid sum guy.

Hannah   She always does that. She's a girl who can't say no my Vicky. I didn't even want to come out west. A guy only has to look at her and she's in there. I'll see her tomorrow, she'll have a big smile on her face. She'll laugh it off like nothing ever happened.

Tone   Then yu'll slap her.

Hannah   That's wat friends are for.

Tone   Cool.

Hannah   No offence right Tone, but you're pretty stupid ain't you?

Tone   Excuse me?

Hannah   How come you didn't talk to me in the club?

Tone   Yu were chattin' to Mal.

Hannah   I was looking at you.

Tone   Shut up.

Hannah   I was.

Tone   Yeah?

Hannah   So what does that tell you?

Tone   Yu were juss lookin'.

Hannah   At you.

Tone   Me?

Hannah   Fuck's sake Tone.

Tone   Wat about Mal?

Hannah   I don't fancy Mal.

Tone   Yu were dancin' wid him.

Hannah   No I wasn't.

Tone   Yu had yer hands all over him.

Hannah   No, he had his hands all over me.

Tone   Nuh man. Yer a prick teaser.

Hannah   What?

Tone   Yu are.

Hannah   Oh forget this.

Tone   Yes or no the trut.

Hannah   You wouldn't know the truth if it bit you on the arse.

Tone   Yu know how many girls I seen Mal wid?

Hannah   Keep hanging round with him and that's all you'll see.

Tone   No.

Hannah *gives* **Tone** *a seriously long kiss.*

Tone (*stunned*)   Yeah?

Hannah   Think about what else you could've had.

Tone   Hold up, ware yer goin'?

Hannah   I'm getting a cab.

Tone   No. Don't.

Hannah   You spinning Tone?

Tone   Like a wheel man.

Hannah   You never been kissed?

Tone   Yes! Is wat yu tink I am?

Hannah   Don't get defensive.

Tone   I ain't. Course I've bin kissed. More than that as well.

Hannah   Check out Mr Stud.

Tone   I have right.

Hannah   I believe you.

Tone   Thass awright den.

Hannah   You've got such beautiful eyes.

Tone (*laughs*)   Rahtid man.

Hannah   Why d'you talk like that?

Tone   It's the way I talk.

Hannah   It's the way he talks.

Tone   I like it.

Spotlight on **Mal** *only, standing in KFC.*

Mal   Chicken breast, I want a chicken breast burger now yer cunt. Yu turn deaf or summin? Fuck the queue, I don't care if yu got queues comin' outta yer arse, I want my burger right? Yu smelly little rass! BURGER! (*Turns round to face the guy behind him.*) Hey brother get yer hand off my jacket awright, get yer hand off my jacket. It costs more than wat yu got on. (*Turns round to the cashier.*) Ware's my

burger? I ain't waitin' in no one's line, get my burger!
Brother! Don't touch me right, not unless yu want me to
bus' yer arse right in front of yer fuckin' gal here. Yeah,
yeah, show me wat yu can do, show me. (*To the cashier.*) Who
the fuck yu lookin' at? Ware's my burger, get me it, now!
(*Turns round.*) Yu wanna do it now, wid yer Listerine
mouthwash breath, come now yer black bastard, come!
(*Pulls out his Stanley knife.*)

Lights down on **Mal**.

Lights back on **Tone** *and* **Hannah**.

Hannah   Let's get a cab back to my place.

Tone   Wat?

Hannah   We can be by ourselves. (*Kisses him again.*)

Tone   I don't believe this.

Hannah   Wat?

Tone   All dis time right, I gone clubbin' wid Mal, standin'
there, watchin' him get nuff girls, nuff pussy, untold! It's
always him tellin' me to go away, disappear.

Hannah   Now it's your turn.

Tone   Juss tell me yu don't fancy Mal fer trut right.

Hannah   Bloody hell.

Tone   Yu don't move in on anoder man's gal Hannah.

Hannah   I ain't his gal.

Tone   Yu really don't fancy him?

Hannah   Tone!

Tone   Sweet bwai!

Hannah   I bloody don't!

Tone   I mean me, I'm a sweet bwai. I can't wait to see his
face when I tell him man.

Hannah   Wat d'you hang round with him for?

Tone   He's my mate, he's my spa.

Hannah   But you don't need him Tone. His lot ain't all that you know. I don't care what they say.

Tone   Wat you mean 'his lot'?

Hannah   You know wat I mean.

Tone   Tell me.

Hannah   They ain't all that Tone, no matter what they say and think. Blacks Tone. That's what I'm talking about.

Tone   Yu a racist.

Hannah   No.

Tone   Yu are ennit? A bloody racist.

Hannah   I just don't hang round with blacks that's all. It's a question of taste.

Tone   Yu best fuck off then. Go get yer cab, move. Ca' if yu don't like Mal, yu don't like me right.

Hannah   You're not black though.

Tone   I might as well be right.

Hannah   Looked in the mirror lately?

Tone   Don't chat like yu know me.

Hannah   You really want to be like Mal? 'Don't fuck wid a bwai and him chicken.' There must be something seriously missing in your life if you think acting like them is going to fill it for you.

Tone   Piss off.

Hannah   You piss off.

Tone   There ain't nuttin' missin' in my life.

Hannah   Ain't there? I know you want to come home with me.

Tone   No I don't.

Hannah   Yes you do.

Tone   Yu ain't nuttin' but a facety bitch right.

Hannah   Stop acting like a prat.

Tone   Runnin' my friend down, expectin' me to take it. Gal yu outta order.

Hannah (*writes her number on a note, stuffs it into his pocket*)   Call me when you've grown up.

Tone *takes the note out and throws it to the ground.*

Hannah   You're a prat Tone. (*Exits.*)

Mal *enters.*

Mal   Yes! Oh yes! 'Bout him wantin' to fuck wid me! Yes! Ware the gal?

Tone   Gone.

Mal   Gone bloody ware?

Tone   Juss gone. Wat 'appened to yu?

Mal   Puttin' sum cunt under manners man. I tek him outside right, drag his bony little arse out on the street, he get me in the face, then I fuckin' get him on the ground man, givin' it to him serious kicks!

Tone   Yu lie!

Mal   It's true. I thought I was gonna kill him bad man, then sum oder cunt pulled me off. I thought it was one of his mates havin' a pop – guess who it was, guess?

Tone   I dunno.

Mal   Delroy!

Tone   Delroy?

Mal   Large as life!

Tone   He's still inside dough.

Mal   Juss come out, las' week. Hear the joke now, he's only turned Muslim.

Tone   Yer mum!

Mal   On my life!

Tone   Delroy?

Mal   Don't Tone, yer juss gonna mek me howl for trut. He wants to take me to a meetin'. (*The boys howl with laughter.*) Remember how we used to look up to him, desperate to join his gang, remember Tone?

Tone   Yeah.

Mal   Look at him now. Him a fool ennit?

Tone   Him a fool Mal.

Mal   'Bout him tell me he got a life.

Tone   Ennit!

Mal   Ennit, ennit, ennit – yer such a fuckin' parrot.

Tone   Come again?

Mal   Ware de gal?

Tone   I told yu she blew us out, took a cab.

Mal   Wat yu say to her?

Tone   Nuttin.

Mal   Yu were chattin' shit to her.

Tone   No.

Mal   Tell me the trut.

Tone   I said no. She were nuttin' but a slag anyhow.

Mal   I know that. Yu tink I stupid or summin? She woulda bin up for both of us, yu woulda got pussy. I wanna poke! There muss be sum place still open. Let's go.

Tone   Whose gonna let yu in wid yer face.

Mal   Yu turn deaf?

Tone   Stop treatin' me like a cunt awright!

Mal   If yu gonna cry, go home and do it. (*Exits.*)

Tone *picks up the note and puts it in his pocket. He follows* **Mal**.

Tone's bedroom. A couple of nights later.

Tone's *porno film is on.* **Mal** *is fast asleep on the bed.* **Carol** *comes in dressed in short black dress and high heels. She is wearing make-up and looking a lot older and more attractive than she did in her last scene.*

Carol   No one's gonna touch me right, well watch me now Tone . . . Mal?

She sees that **Mal** *is asleep. She finds his jacket and covers him with it. She then leans over and gives him a soft peck on the cheek.* **Mal** *begins to wake up.* **Carol** *leans back quickly.*

Carol   Sorry.

Mal (*wakes up*)   Carol?

Carol   Yeah. I didn't mean to . . .

Mal   (*still dazed*) Wat time is it?

Carol   Half eight.

Mal   Half eight! I thought it was later.

Carol   Nuh.

Mal *notices that the porno film is still on. He is clearly embarrassed as he searches around the bed for the remote.*

Carol It's awright, I've seen it twice. They both jump into the pool after this and she bites his dick off. (*Notices* **Mal** *is looking at her.*) Wat?

Mal Carol, wat yu got on?

Carol A dress.

Mal Says who?

Carol Nice ennit?

Mal Jesus!

Carol Ware's Tone?

Mal Out.

Carol Wat 'appened to yer face?

Mal Cut myself shavin'.

Carol And the rest.

Mal Shoulda seen the oder bloke. Geezer asked for it.

Carol And yu gave it to him.

Mal Yep.

Carol He gave yu summin an all.

Mal I'm awright.

Carol Yer always seem to be fightin' these days.

Mal So wat?

Carol Yer gonna get mash up.

Mal No.

Carol (*notices* **Mal** *is still staring*) Yu like my dress then Mal?

Mal I've seen it before.

Carol I know yu have.

Mal On Linsey.

Carol   Yu got a good memory.

Mal   It's hard to ferget.

Carol   I'm one of her sisters now! Don't laugh. We're goin' to sum rave tonight.

Mal   Yu should be doin' yer homework yer bad little girl.

Carol   I ain't little.

Mal   Wat rave yu goin' to?

Carol   Sum place down Wembley.

Mal   Wembley! Carol listen to me, that dress only says one ting yer nuh.

Carol   Good.

Mal   Yu want every horny geezer chasin' yer?

Carol   I wanna enjoy myself.

Mal   Stay at home.

Carol   Don't be such a lightweight.

Mal   Do yer homework.

Carol   No.

Mal   Read a book or summin, but don't do this.

Carol   No one wants me to grow up.

Mal   Ca' it ain't worth it.

Carol   I ain't pissin' me life away, I juss wanna bitta fun.

Mal   Yu ain't ready.

Carol   I am.

Mal   Wat, wat yu ready for?

Carol   Everything. Yu don't believe me?

Mal   Never mind, ferget it.

Carol Yer nose is bleedin'.

Mal Don't worry about it.

Carol Yer such a hard man. (*Puts a tissue to his face.*)

Mal Leave it.

Carol Shut up.

Mal *looks away, trying very hard not to look at her cleavage.*

Carol Wat?

Mal Any guys give yu trouble right, I go cut them for yer.

Carol Can't yu get enough of it awready?

Mal No.

Carol My hero.

Mal I'm serious.

Carol Yer poor mum man.

Mal Poor mum nuttin. She's a stupid cow.

Carol Least she cares about yer.

Mal Did care.

Carol Say again?

Mal Ain't Tone told yer? Threw me out ennit? Come back when I'm grown up – fuckin' tellin' me wat to do.

Carol Ware yer stayin' then?

Mal Here for tonight, then I'll see. Don't worry about it, I'll find sumware.

Carol Wat if yu can't, ware yu gonna go?

Mal Dunno.

Carol Who's gonna look after yer?

Mal I'll look after myself Carol.

Carol   Yeah but she can't throw yu out like that Mal.

Mal   She awready has man.

Carol   Yeah but she can't, not when yer . . .

Mal   When I'm wat?

Carol   Nuttin.

Mal   When I'm wat? Wat Carol? Tell me right!

Carol   Yer sick ennit.

Mal   Who told yu I was sick?

Carol   Yu can't juss go. Yu can't.

Mal   Who told yer I was sick?

Carol   No one.

Mal   So wat yu chattin' about then? Who told yu I was bloody sick Carol?

Carol   Yer mum. I overheard her and my mum chattin' about it.

Mal   She was talkin' about me to yer mum?

Carol   Yeah.

Mal   The fuckin' bitch. She juss can't leave it alone can she? She has to open her mout whenever she feel.

Carol   She's worried about yer.

Mal   Deh's nuttin to worry about dough.

Carol   She says yer scared Mal.

Mal   When yu ever known me to be scared Carol?

Carol   Yu won't go to the doctor. She don't know wat to do.

Mal   Yu musta bin doin' sum serious eavesdroppin' to hear all that.

Carol   I didn't mean to.

Mal   Wat is it about my life yu find so fascinatin'?

Carol   Don't shout at me. I'm sorry awright.

Mal (*kisses her without thinking*)   That was a bad idea.

Carol   Do it again if yu like.

Mal   That'll be anoder bad idea.

Carol   Why?

Mal   No. Listen to me yeah, don't tell anyone about me right.

Carol   Course I won't.

Mal   Don't tell Tone.

Carol   He's yer mate dough.

Mal   Yeah but all he knows about, Carol, is havin' a laugh, ennit? It's wat we all do. Fuck about, we don't know nuttin' about anything serious, we don't wanna know. If I tell him I got leukaemia, yu watch his face, goin' all funny and that. Starin' at me, not knowin' wat to say, no laughin', juss gonna stand around like an idiot, waitin' fer me to die.

Carol   Die? Wat yu mean die?

Mal   I didn't mean that.

Carol   Yer not gonna die.

Mal   I know I ain't.

Carol   So why say it then? Don't be so stupid.

Mal   Wat yu bloody know, 'bout me stupid. Wat I've got is bad Carol right, I might need wat dem call a bone marrow transplant yeah, from anoder black guy.

Carol   There yu go then, case rested, yer ain't gonna die.

Mal   There ain't enough blacks on the register dough Carol, there ain't enough. Cos they don't give a shit.

Carol   I don't care, I don't bloody care Mal.

Mal   I'm gonna kill my mum when I see her next.

Carol   Yu ain't gonna die right.

Mal   Yu tink I wanna?

Carol   So wat do yu wan'?

Mal   I wanna be white.

Carol   White?

Mal   Yer so lucky.

Carol   Lucky?

Mal   Can't yu see that?

Carol *puts her hands on his shoulder.*

Mal   Don't.

Carol   Why?

Mal   Go to yer party Carol.

Carol   I wanna stay.

Mal   Carol.

Carol   I don't wanna go.

Mal   Yer juss like yer broder man.

Carol   Oh cheers.

Mal   Yu don't listen. (*Kisses her.*)

Carol   Don't stop right. Don't bloody stop.

The kids' playground. A few weeks later.

Mal *and* **Tone** *are both eating chips.*

Mal   Oh man, that was a concert yu nuh!

Tone   Public Enemy!

Mal   They were bad ennit?

Tone   Untold.

Mal   Told yu they were.

Tone   No I told yu.

Mal   Shut up man I told yu.

Tone   Who paid for the tickets?

Mal   Who lent yu the money?

Tone   I'll pay yu back.

Mal   Yu fish.

Tone   Move, yer blood clart.

Mal   Move, yer batay bwai!

Tone/Mal   Wat de rass! (*Laughs.*)

Tone   First thing tomorrow I go buy their new CD. Public Enemy! (*Dances.*)

Mal   Sit down before someone sees yer. (*Throws a chip at him.*)

Tone   Move. Wat's bloody keepin' her? Chips gettin' cold man.

Mal   So eat 'em.

Tone   Can't eat chips without tomato sauce, wass the matter wid her?

Mal   Starve then. (*Throws another chip at him.*)

Tone   Yu wanna die?

Mal   Come.

Tone *opens his bag of chips and returns fire. The boys continue to throw chips at one another until one of Tone's finally hits* **Mal**.

Tone   Yes! I got the mother in my sights and I mash him up.

Mal   Lucky shot.

Tone   Oh juss take it like a man will yer?

Mal   Rematch.

Tone   No, I'm hungry.

Mal   Yu ain't got any sauce.

Tone   Fuck the sauce I'm hungry man. I swear she takes the piss. Chippie is two minutes away and she takes half an hour.

Mal   See that girl in the row in front of us Tone?

Tone   Which one?

Mal   White T-shirt, tight jeans. Looks like Shaznay from All Saints. Fit bitch. She was givin' me the eye.

Tone   How yu know it weren't me?

Mal   Yer mum.

Tone   She was wid sum guy dough.

Mal   See the way he was lookin' over, tryin' to size me up.

Tone   Didn't see yu do anyting.

Mal   Thass the idea. (*Produces a piece of paper.*) 0181 605 7894.

Tone   Yu joke!

Mal   Name, Gina!

Tone   How yer get it man?

Mal   She slipped me it when I went for a slash. Am I top, or am I top?

Tone   She got a boyfriend Mal.

Mal   Yer point?

Tone   He look useful.

Mal   Yer point?

Tone   Yu wanna get mash up?

Mal   I'm on a roll man.

Tone   Watever.

Mal   Awright den, yu don't wan' me to ask if she's got a friend, I won't ask.

Tone   Did I say that? Did those words leave my lips?

Mal   Yu can't wait to get yer sack emptied.

Tone   How yu know I ain't?

Mal   Yer mum.

Tone   Watever.

Mal   Wat yu smilin' about?

Tone   Nuttin.

Carol *enters. She throws* **Tone** *a packet of tomato ketchup.*

Carol   Yu happy now? Get it yerself next time.

Tone   Shut yer legs.

Carol   Ware my chips?

Tone   Up my arse.

Carol   Yu greedy sod.

Tone *burps in her face.*

Carol   Piss off! I really fancied sum chips man.

Tone   Errgh, she fancies a chip. (*The boys laugh.*) Yu wanna suck one off ennit?

Carol   Yer so childish it's untrue.

Tone   I bet yu don't ring that girl Mal.

Mal   Shut up man.

Tone   Shut up wat, yu gonna ring her yes or no?

Mal   Don't worry about it.

Carol   Wat girl?

Tone   One wid bigger tits than yours.

Carol   Fuck off and die Tone.

Tone   I'm goin' for a slash.

Carol   Like yu got summin to slash with?

Tone   Oh thass so hurtful Carol, I can feel the bruises. Please don't call me any more names Carol, please. Help me Mal. (*Exits.*)

Carol   He's such a wazzock.

Mal   He ain't so bad.

Carol   He never gives me a fag.

Mal   Yer too young.

Carol   Yer aways sayin' that. Wat girl?

Mal   Ferget it.

Carol   It was that slapper at the concert weren't it?

Mal   No.

Carol   The one who couldn't keep her eyes off yu, don't lie. How can yu fancy that?

Mal   I don't.

Carol   She was fat.

Mal   She weren't fat.

Carol   She could pick up a table wid her arse.

Mal   Wat yu stressin' for Carol?

Carol   I'm not. I don't blame her fancyin' yu, who wouldn't fancy yer? Yu fancy me?

Mal   Course.

Carol   Yu love me?

Mal   Yes!

Carol   Please don't dump me Mal.

Mal   Who said I was?

Carol   I'm gonna look after yu. We're gonna look after each other.

Mal   Yeah yeah.

Carol   Yu never take me seriously.

Mal   Don't go on.

Carol   Come on Mal, let's tell everyone about us.

Mal   Yer mad.

Carol   Why not?

Mal   Too soon man.

Carol   Yu aways say that as well.

Mal   Wass the rush?

Carol   There's no rush, it's juss doin' my head in. I'm goin' out wid the fittest, best-lookin' bwai on the whole estate and I can't tell anyone he's mine.

Mal   Wat am I, a trophy or summin?

Carol   No. But I really wanted to hold yer hand tonight, but I couldn't cos Tone might be watchin'. And I've seen the way Linsey and the other girls look at yu. It gets me mad. I wanna cut 'em up man, tell them hands off.

Mal   Ca' yu love me right?

Carol   Yeah.

Mal   Suck my finger den.

Carol   (*sucks his finger*)   Anywhere else?

Mal   Yu had to do it ennit?

Carol   Wat?

Mal   Carry on like sum little tart. Why yu love it so much?

Carol   I'm only messin'.

Mal   'Bout yu love me.

Carol   I do. Yu can't dump me Mal.

Mal   I can do wat I want right.

Carol   I wanna be wid yu. More than yu realise.

Mal   Wat yu chattin' about now?

Carol   Remember when we did it in our livin' room?

Mal   Carol?

Carol   On the sofa.

Mal   Keep yer voice down.

Carol   Best one ever that was.

Mal   Wass the matter wid yu?

Carol   We made a baby.

Mal   Wat the fuck yu talkin' about?

Carol   I'm late.

Mal   Don't chat shit to me Carol.

Carol   I ain't.

Mal   Wat yu bloody mean we made a baby? Fuck off!

Carol   I didn't mean for it to happen Mal, I swear to God, but I don't care any more, I don't. Ca' I reckon it's gonna be awright.

Mal   No Carol, it's not awright.

Carol   I wanna be wid yu.

Mal   And this is how yu do it?

Carol   Yu said yu wanted to be different. Well I want to be different as well now. I love yu.

Mal   Gettin' yerself pregnant man, yu stupid bitch.

Carol   Don't shout at me.

Mal   Wat the fuck's the matter wid yu?

Carol   Mal?

Mal   Get off me, juss get away from me. How do I know it's mine?

Carol   It is yours.

Mal   How do yu know? I bet yu've had a whole heap of traffic goin' through yu.

Carol   No.

Mal   Yes yu mean, 'bout no.

Carol   Mal!

Mal   Yu stay away from me right. Yu don't come near me, yu don't even talk to me. Ca' yu ain't nuttin' but a fuckin' little whore. (*Exits.*)

Tone *comes back out.*

Tone   Carol! Yu bin smokin' spliff in my room again? Don't lie right. Mum juss found a joint under my pillow and I know it ain't mine. Why can't yu smoke it in yer room, wass the matter wid yer? Ware's Mal? Carol? Wat yu cryin' for? Wass 'appened, Carol? Wat yu cryin' for?

The kids' playground, a few days later.

Tone *comes out of his flat. The sound of* **Carol** *and* **Tone**'s *mum yelling.* **Tone** *slams the door behind him. He sits on the swing and lights a cigarette.* **Hannah** *creeps up and covers his eyes.*

Hannah   Give us a snog.

Tone   Wat yu doin' here?

Hannah   Nice way to greet me.

Tone   I told yer, I can't come out tonight.

Hannah   I've missed you. Want to show me your bedroom again?

Tone   Yu mad?

Hannah   Don't talk like that.

Tone   I can't Hannah.

Hannah   Well if you're not interested . . .

Tone   I am interested.

Hannah   You can go fuck yourself.

Tone   I can't take yu in, cos it's like a bloody war in there.

Hannah   Carol?

Tone   She juss told Mum.

Hannah   She go mad?

Tone   Nuclear. Then me mum starts blamin' me, they're doin' my head in.

Hannah   It should be somebody else's head you should be doing in.

Tone   Leave it.

Hannah   He's out of order Tone.

Tone   I don't know it's him for sure.

Hannah   Did I hear you say that?

Tone   Yu ain't seen the way she's bin lately, puttin' it about, gaggin' for it.

Hannah   Show some respect will you? You should be helping her, not slagging her off. I bet yu ain't even spoken to him or nothing, have you?

Tone   How can I when I ain't seen him for weeks?

Hannah   That's an excuse.

Tone   Wat yu wan' me to do?

Hannah   Find him.

Tone   I don't know ware he is. It's like he's disappeared.

Hannah   You soft git. You still care about him.

Tone   No.

Hannah   Even after what he's done.

Tone   I don't.

Hannah   I don't know what I saw in you.

Tone   Don't yer? I do.

Hannah   Don't flatter yourself Tone.

Tone   I was good weren't I?

Hannah   Whatever.

Tone   Wat yu mean watever? Watever don't come into it.

Hannah   We're supposed to be talking about Carol here.

Tone   Fuck Carol. She's my sister not yours. I was good weren't I?

Hannah   You're a wild animal Tone.

Tone   Don't take the piss.

Hannah   Oh get a life.

Tone   Yu don't like it yu know wat yu can do.

Hannah   You're the one who called me, Tone, remember?

Tone   Juss tell me I was good.

Hannah   Yes you were good. Yer a bad bwai! Is this what you and Mal do, compare notes? Did he brag about your sister to you?

Tone   Shut yer mouth Hannah.

Hannah   Mal and your sister, your sister and Mal, Mal taking your sister's knickers off.

Tone   Shut up right!

Hannah   You want to hit someone, hit Mal.

Tone   I will when I see him, awright, happy? I hate the bastard Hannah.

Hannah   Black bastard.

Tone   Wat?

Hannah   Call him a black bastard.

Tone   Wat yu sayin', why would I wanna do that?

Hannah   Cos you want to. Cos it was the first thing that came into your head. You've always wanted to say it Tone, be honest. I bet yer mum's said it a thousand times this morning. You say you hate him, prove it.

Tone   Yer fuckin' mad.

Hannah   Prove it Tone.

Tone   No.

Hannah   Bye.

Tone   We bin mates from time.

Hannah   So that means he can do what he wants, screw yer little sister?

Tone   No.

Hannah   Cos thass wat yer sayin'.

Tone   It ain't.

Hannah   Prove it then. Say it. I remember when I first said it. There was this black girl I had to work with once, right stroppy cow she was. Coming in every day late with this attitude they all have, rude to the customers, wouldn't stop, she started on me, really aggressive. I just turned and snapped 'You don't like your job, piss off back to the dole queue, you moody black bitch.' I couldn't believe it. I didn't mean to say it, it just came out. But it felt so good Tone.

Tone   Watever.

Hannah   We don't have to like them Tone. That is allowed.

Tone   I wish I never met yu.

Hannah   You ain't got nothing to be jealous about Tone, yer better than him. (*Kisses him.*) You're my wild animal.

Mal *enters.*

Mal   Awright Tone?

Hannah   Look who it is.

Tone   Wat yu doin' here?

Mal   Wass 'appenin'?

Tone   I thought yer mum kicked yu out.

Mal   I come for sum of my things is that awright wid yu? So wass 'appenin'?

Hannah   You got some front.

Mal   Quiet horse.

Hannah   You what?

Mal   Wat yu doin' Tone?

Hannah   What d'you call me?

Mal   Earth callin' Tone.

Hannah   Tell him Tone.

Mal   Wass she doin' here? Yu mekin' moves? Sly man!

Hannah   Tone!

Mal   Wat yu doin' man?

Tone   Yu seen Carol?

Mal   Should I have?

Tone   Yu tell me Mal.

Mal   Wat is this?

Hannah   Don't act like you don't know.

Mal   Is who ask yu?

Tone   Yu make me sick.

Mal   She was givin' it to me on a plate, wat was I supposed to do?

Hannah   Hit him Tone.

Mal   Let him try. It was pussy man.

Tone   She was my sister.

Mal   She's still pussy.

Tone *takes a swing at him.*

Hannah   Hit him!

Mal (*holding him down*)   Yu think we're still at school? Yu want me to bus' yer head? (*Lets him go.*)

Hannah   I'll get some help.

Mal   Yeah yu go get his mum.

Tone   Leave it.

Hannah   He's going mental, I ain't staying here with him.

Tone   So go then! Juss go Hannah.

Hannah   Awright. Ring me when you get home. (*Exits.*)

Mal   Lipsin up a girl behind my back? Yer learnin' bwai.

Tone   Yer a bastard.

Mal   Laters.

Tone   Yer supposed to be my friend man.

Mal   Wass that matter?

Tone   Yu went behind my back, thass wat matters. If yu fancied her, yu shoulda said summin.

Mal   I don't fancy her.

Tone   So why yu do it?

Mal   She was wearin' Linsey Evans's dress Tone. The one I told yu about, the short black one. She looked good in it, her arse was all nice and fit man, wat was I supposed to do? Am I a batay bwai? Don't tell me yu wouldn't do the same if she weren't yer sister.

Tone   She's nuttin but a kid man.

Mal   She shouldn't have bin playin' then, yu shoulda bin lookin' out for her.

Tone   My mum's gonna cut yer head off.

Mal   Yu think I care wat yer mum wants to do? When pussy's on offer yu tek it! Fuck wat matters thass it!

Tone   Even if it's Carol? Wass she ever do to yu?

Mal   So it's awright for me to shag Nicole, we have a big laugh about that, but not yer precious little sister.

Tone   Nicole's the same age as yu.

Mal   I don't bloody care right.

Tone   So thass it then?

Mal   Yep.

Tone   You fuckin' . . .

Mal Wat?

Tone Black bastard.

Mal Yeah, keep it comin'.

Tone Nigger!

Mal Yes! Thass wat I am, and niggers don't care Tone, it's not in us. I mean we'd rather stuff our faces wid fried chicken, go out and tief, fuck whoever we like, than give blood to one of our own who badly needs it – who could die if he don't get it.

Tone Wat yu talkin' about?

Mal We do wat everyone thinks, wat everyone expects, so give 'em wat they want, go for the pussy.

Tone Wat yu mean 'bout people givin' blood Mal?

Mal I'm talkin 'bout pussy right?

Tone Are yu sick or summin?

Mal No.

Tone Stop treatin' me like a cunt Mal.

Mal Stop actin' like a cunt. Yu wanna be black or not? Yes or no?

Tone No.

Mal Don't follow me then.

Tone Don't worry. Yu tink I wanna end up like yu?

Mal Move.

Tone She could do yu for rape.

Mal Bitch was gaggin' fer it.

Tone I'm gonna fuckin' kill yu.

Mal Come!

Tone *walks away.*

Mal   Gwan then, juss walk away Tone, walk away. Ca' it's easy for yu ennit? Ennit? Wat about me yer cunt?

Tone   Yu got wat yu wanted.

Mal   Wat yu know wat I want? Maybe I wanted to stay out here, fly aeroplanes wid Rich.

Tone   Rich?

Mal   Wat, yu ferget who he is now?

Tone   No.

Mal   Yu bastard man.

Tone   Yeah like I'm really gonna forget him ain't I Mal?

Mal   Guilty conscience?

Tone   Piss off.

Mal   It was yu that did it Tone.

Tone   Fuck off was it.

Mal   It was.

Tone   Yu blamin' me, after all this time? Get over it will yer, he killed himself.

Mal   Yu made him.

Tone   We both made him. Yu and me. Wat d'yer bring this up for? Wass the matter wid yu? Yer sick in the head man, is that where it is?

Mal   Get the fuck outta my face.

Tone   Fuck yu! (*Exits.*)

The kids' playground. Lights on **Rich, Young Mal** *and* **Young Tone**. **Mal** *is watching them.*

Young Mal   Dog.

Rich *crawls around the floor, barking like a dog.*

Young Mal   Pig.

Rich, *still crawling, squeals like a pig.*

Young Tone   Do a lion.

Rich *roars.*

Mal (*to* **Young Mal**)   Stop it.

Young Mal   Do a monkey.

Young Tone   Yeah monkey, do it!

Rich *does a monkey while the boys rifle through his bag.*

Young Tone   Yu better have money for me today, I'm not jokin'. (*Finds a paper aeroplane.*) Wat a loner.

Rich   Gimme that.

Young Mal   Who told yu to stop?

Rich   I want my plane back.

Young Mal/Young Tone *laugh.*

Rich   I want my plane back.

Young Tone   So come get it. Come on!

He holds the plane in the air as **Rich** *tries to reach for it, hitting out in desperation.*

Wanna fight me do yer Rich?

Young Mal   Go on Rich fight him.

Young Tone   Come on then. (*Clips him around the head.*) Oh yes Tyson's in control here, his opponent don't know wat day it is, and anoder, and anoder.

Young Mal   Yu little spas Rich.

Mal   Shut up.

Young Mal   Yu ain't nuttin' man.

Mal   Leave him alone.

Young Tone (*wins the fight. He laughs.*)   See that? I beat up a black kid man, me one Tone! Ennit?

Young Mal   He ain't black. Fuck knows wat he is.

Young Tone   Come.

The boys run off, but not before **Young Mal** *tears the plane up.* **Rich** *gets up, trying to piece it back together.*

Mal (*finding another piece*)   Sorry Rich.

Rich   Wat for, yu got wat yu want.

Mal   This ain't wat I want.

Rich   It don't matter.

Mal   Don't go, stay.

Rich   I wanna go home.

Mal   Stay Rich.

Rich   Let me go. I wanna go home.

Mal   Yer not goin' home, I know wat yer goin' to do.

Rich   Wat am I gonna do Mal?

Mal   Juss stay awright.

Rich   It's too late.

Mal   Stop doin' this to me.

Rich   Doin' wat?

Mal   All this.

Rich   It ain't me it's yu.

Mal   I don't wanna remember.

Rich   Don't then.

Mal   Yer makin' me.

Rich   Wat yu want me to do Mal?

Mal   Why d'yu do it?

Rich   Did wat? I fell. Thass wat yu told everyone.

Mal   I couldn't tell the trut, me and Tone woulda bin in nuff shit.

Rich   Yeah, yu and Tone.

Mal   Yu killed yerself for nuttin.

Rich   If I ain't better than a white kid, then I'm nuttin. It's wat yu said.

Mal   I was talkin' bollocks.

Rich   Yu didn't think it was bollocks when yu said it.

Mal   I do now.

Rich   Only cos yu think yer dyin'.

Mal   I am.

Rich   Yer so stupid.

Mal   If I could peel this skin right off me, every last inch yu know. I'm sorry.

Rich   Stop sayin' that.

Mal   We shoulda bin friends.

Rich   We were.

Mal   We shoulda bin friends now.

He tries to make an aeroplane out of the small piece of paper he has, but is having little success. **Rich** *watches him. Finally,* **Rich** *offers him a fresh sheet of paper and he begins folding.*

Wass it like?

Rich   Wat?

Mal   Bein' dead?

Rich   It don't feel like anything.

Mal   Good.

Rich   I didn't say it was good. Yu miss things.

Mal   I'm scared man, wat do I do?

Rich   Yu get on ennit.

Mal   Yer a big help.

Rich   Wat do yu want me to say?

Mal   Wat if I can't get on?

Rich   Yu have to. (*Points to Mal's plane.*) Wings!

Mal   Awright. (*Carries on folding.*) Sound like my mum. Hey, look at this man. (*The finished plane looks good.*) Look, fuckin' hell!

Rich   Fly it then.

Mal (*flies the plane, laughs*)   Cool! Wanna fly them through yer window like we used to?

Rich   No.

Mal   Come on, race yu up there.

Rich   I dunno.

Mal   Rich?

Rich   Awright, one, two . . . (*Runs up.*)

Mal   Oi! I'm the one that does that.

The kids' playground.

Tone *is alone in the playground, smoking.* **Carol** *creeps up behind him, her pregnancy is starting to show. She grabs* **Tone** *from behind. He jumps.*

Tone   Yu stupid cow.

Carol   Gimme a fag.

Tone   Yer not . . .

Carol   (*finishes*) . . . yer not allowed. Yer such a parrot.

Tone   And yer a fat bitch, deal wid it. Ware yu goin'?

Carol   Chemist.

Tone   Good, get me a bag of chips while yer out there.

Carol   Am I yer slave?

Tone   And a saveloy.

Carol   Wass it worth?

Tone   Yer 'avin' a laugh.

Carol   Juss one fag.

Tone   Piss off.

Carol   Grandad.

Mal *enters.*

Carol (*eyes him*)   I was wonderin' wat the smell was.

Mal   Oh that hurt Carol, I can feel the bruises.

Carol   Back wid yer mummy then?

Mal   Got a problem?

Carol   Yu best stay away from me right.

Mal   Juss move.

Carol (*about to cry*)   Swivel Mal. (*Exits.*)

Mal   Get a life. (*To* **Tone**) Yu got summin to say?

Tone   Ware yer goin'? Hospital?

Mal   Yu a copper?

Tone   Carol told me. How come yu didn't?

Mal   Cos I didn't feel like it.

Tone   Yu awright then?

Mal   Yes! I juss gotta go for tests and that.

Tone   If it were me man.

Mal   Yu ain't me.

Tone   I know I'm juss sayin', if it were me. I'd go mad.

Mal   No shit?

Tone   Yu need help?

Mal   Wat can yu do?

Tone   I dunno. Give blood?

Mal *laughs*.

Tone   Wass so funny? Wat if I saved yer life, yu won't be laughin' then.

Mal   It ain't gonna happen dough.

Tone   How d'yu know?

Mal   Ca' yu ain't black. Yu don't know nuttin man.

Tone   Dumb white Tone, thass me ennit?

Mal   Wat, yu gonna grovel now?

Tone   I don't grovel right.

Mal   Yu should be beatin' the shit outta me.

Tone   I can't dough can I?

Mal   Go on take a punch. I won't do nuttin. I'll juss stand and let yer. Call me a nigger.

Tone   No.

Mal   It's wat I am.

Tone   Yer not.

Mal   A cocky coon who got his dues.

Tone   Yer mad.

Mal   It's how I feel sumtimes.

Tone   Yu come juss like Hannah.

Mal   She's right.

Tone   No. I'm dumpin' it.

Mal   Yu dump a girl?

Tone   Yu got a problem wid that?

Mal   I bet yu ain't even poked it yet.

Tone   Yeah!

Mal   Lie.

Tone   On my life.

Mal   Go there!

Tone   Ennit.

Mal   But I'd get a few more pokes in if I were yu. I mean it might be a long time before yu get any more.

Tone   Yer mum. I'll get loads right.

The boys manage slight smiles. **Mal** *tries hard to hide his laughter.*

Wat?

Mal   Hate me Tone. Wass the matter wid yu? Don't follow me no more. (*Exits.*)

Tone *watches his friend leave. He finishes his cigarette, and follows him.*

Blackout.